TRADITIONS OF MEDIEVAL ENGLISH DRAMA

English and European Literature

Editor

JOHN LAWLOR

Professor of English
in the University of Keele

'The Crucifixion' from the Wakefield Towneley Cycle of Mystery Plays, presented by the St Neots Players at Ely in 1973

TRADITIONS OF MEDIEVAL
ENGLISH DRAMA

Stanley J. Kahrl

Director of the Center for
Medieval and Renaissance Studies,
Ohio State University

HUTCHINSON UNIVERSITY LIBRARY
LONDON

HUTCHINSON & CO (*Publishers*) LTD
3 Fitzroy Square, London W1

London Melbourne Sydney Auckland
Wellington Johannesburg Cape Town
and agencies throughout the world

First published 1974
© Stanley J. Kahrl 1974

This book has been set in Bembo
Printed in Great Britain by
William Clowes & Sons, Limited
London, Beccles and Colchester

ISBN 0 09 119260 9 (cased)
0 09 119261 7 (paper)

TO JUDY
who went to York first

CONTENTS

PREFACE

Any attempt to provide a general account of English drama in the
fifteenth and sixteenth centuries undertaken at the present moment
must be, in many respects, tentative. So much of what we have 'known'
since E. K. Chambers completed his history of the medieval theatre
has come unstuck. It is not the factual data that Chambers collected
so patiently, under such difficult conditions, that no longer provides a
secure basis for reconstructing the past. More factual information has
appeared in the seventy years since *The Mediaeval Stage* appeared, to
be sure. But the discovery of new material has not often brought with
it startling revisions. What has changed is the superstructure of hypo-
theses upon which Chambers, Karl Young in *The Drama of the Medieval
Church*, and, following them, Hardin Craig in *English Religious
Drama of the Middle Ages*, arranged and ordered that factual data.

The process of revision properly began with H. C. Gardiner's restudy of the reasons for the eventual disappearance of civic religious
drama in England. That study, entitled *Mysteries' End*, appearing in
1946, proposed that the religious drama sponsored by the towns and
villages of late medieval England did not, as Chambers believed, die
like a dinosaur because it had outlived its time, but that it was killed
by the Protestant divines of Elizabeth for political reasons. If Father
Gardiner's thesis is granted, then the drama of late medieval England
should be studied as potentially vital and effective throughout its life,
not as a curious relic of a dead past.[1] Subsequently F. M. Salter, in his
Alexander lectures on *Mediaeval Drama in Chester*, published in 1955,
presented the results of an extensive restudy of local dramatic activity

1. Superior figures refer to Notes, pp. 136–53.

in Chester which led Salter to a sharply increased respect for the civic
drama of that city during the late Middle Ages. However, probably
the most influential single contribution to the dismantling of the superstructure of theory built up of the past was that provided by O. B.
Hardison, Jr, in the opening chapter of *Christian Rite and Christian
Drama*, in which he laid out for inspection the unexamined evolutionary assumptions implicit in all three early accounts of the 'growth'
of medieval drama.

Virtually every account of the early development of European
drama that has appeared based on such accounts as that of Chambers
describes the process of development as an evolutionary one, in which
the plays, often apparently with an organic life of their own, have
grown from simple (i.e., one-celled) origins in playlets worked into
the liturgical practices of the early medieval church to large-scale
productions presented in the naves of cathedrals, then to larger, possibly 'freer' (that is, funnier), open-air productions in the graveyards
surrounding the churches and cathedrals, and thence finally to fully-
grown organisms produced by secular groups in such secular surroundings as the marketplace or guildhall. Finally, dinosaurlike, to use
again a Darwinian example, the drama of the medieval period atro-
phied and died, a victim of a changing environment. Hardison, re-
arranging the texts collected by Karl Young according to their most
probable dates, indicated how often it happens that a most complex
dramatic production precedes in time a simpler form. Furthermore,
once the impulse to create dramatic embodiments of central points in
Christian belief had taken a firm hold, virtually all possible dramatic
forms that were to be exploited throughout the medieval period were
created by conscious artists in a relatively short span of time. Hardison,
like Gardiner and Salter, provided further reason to treat the surviving
dramatic texts as worth serious study.

It is not my purpose to rearrange the factual data concerning the
origins of medieval drama in England onto a new structure designed
to represent more truly the actual development of that drama. This
task has been undertaken by Richard Axton in a separate book in this
series. Rather it is my intention to present a set of model approaches
to the drama of England in the fifteenth and sixteenth centuries.
These approaches depend on the growing body of scholarship and
criticism which has appeared since the three works of revision already
cited, all of it taking as given the assumption that study of early English
drama is an activity rewarding in its own right. An increased number

of anthologies of early drama testify to the growing audience for these plays; an audience stimulated in part by the stage revivals of the past twenty years. Members of that audience are invited to test the validity of the approaches offered in this book on plays of their own choosing if the approaches are found to be rewarding; if they lead to more intelligent readings of plays that are not discussed, then the effort will have been worthwhile.

I wish to acknowledge particularly the support and encouragement of Derek Brewer, who first suggested the need for such a book, Richard Axton, for his thoughtful suggestions in the planning stages, and John Lawlor, for offering me the chance to undertake the task. Also I am indebted to the many scholars attending the discussions on medieval drama in a seminar by that title held during the annual meeting of the Modern Language Association of America. There, in an atmosphere of shared ideas and new discoveries I have been able to mature the thoughts in this book among colleagues who have stood for the best traditions of scholarship. That atmosphere was created by Arnold Williams, the founder of the seminar. To him, and to his enthusiasm for medieval English drama, I shall always be indebted.

I

LOCATING THE PLAYS IN SPACE AND TIME

Among the art forms which characterized the cultural life of England in the later Middle Ages, none so fully embodies the tastes and expectations of the popular audience of those times as does English medieval drama. Not only is this drama an admirable index to the popular cultural life of the times in which it reached its full flower, but also it possesses, as does all great drama, the capacity to move a modern audience as effectively as it moved the audience for which it was written. Modern productions in a variety of places in both England and America have demonstrated over and over again the power of this drama to hold an audience enthralled. Yet despite a century of scholarly effort, it is still difficult to describe for a modern audience who have experienced the power of this drama in a modern production, or to explain to someone who has just read one of the plays for the first time, exactly how the drama of medieval England was actually produced in its original state.

I have stood before Lincoln Cathedral, imagining the scene on a bright July day when the plays of that city were being set forth. I can imagine the crowds milling out beyond the great west gate of the close, buying food and drink from booths set up in the square between the cathedral close and the castle. I can imagine the crowd inside the close looking up at the great west front of the cathedral, with its frieze portraying the Fall of Man, or Noah and his ark, and then turning to watch these events enacted before their eyes. But how? On scaffold stages or on movable wagons bearing elaborate sets? Arranged in a circle, or in a semi-circle? With the crowd surrounding them, packed in on all sides, or with a large open acting area in the centre? I cannot complete the picture, for the surviving accounts of the drama of Lincoln in the fifteenth and sixteenth centuries do not provide enough specific information to permit me to do so.

Or take another example of a play about which we do not know enough. In a manuscript known as the Macro manuscript, after the name of a former owner, Cox Macro, occurs one of the more ambitious medieval English plays, *The Castle of Perseverance*. This play is preceded by the earliest known illustration in England indicating how a play was to be staged.[1] The drawing shows a stylized castle with a bed under it, inside a ring which represents either a ditch filled with water 'if any dyche may be mad[e]', or else a fence of some sort. Outside the ring are locations for five scaffolds, four on the compass points and the fifth, for Covetous, in the north-east, between the scaffolds for God and Belial. The hero, Mankind, dies in the bed under the castle at the foot of which is Covetous' cupboard; the plan also indicates the costumes for the four Daughters of God who debate Mankind's ultimate fate. Finally, the plan notes that Belial is to have pipes filled with burning gunpowder 'in hys handys and in hys erys and in hys ars whanne he gothe to batayl'.[2]

Richard Southern, in 1957, published a seminal book devoted entirely to a reconstruction of the manner of performance of *The Castle of Perseverance*, relying not only on the drawing, but also on the stage directions and internal evidence of the play itself. The book, entitled *The Medieval Theatre in the Round*, drew on his wide experience in the modern theatre. One would have thought that the problem of visualizing a production of this play as originally produced was settled. Not at all. In his reconstruction, Southern proposed that the scaffolds, which in the drawing were placed outside the ring, were actually inside it. Why? Because Southern posited that the ring actually represented a ditch intended to keep out non-paying customers. If one has a ditch, one has to get rid of the dirt which was in the ditch, *ergo* we must have an embankment inside the ditch, on top of which are to be located the scaffolds. Such embankments do exist in Cornwall, where they are called 'rounds'. As a recent production of the surviving Cornish version of a Corpus Christi cycle indicates, such rounds are in fact good theatres. Internal references to hills within the text of *The Castle of Perseverance* would seem to substantiate Southern's thesis. Thus, despite the clear evidence of the picture, many of those discussing the play now take it as given that the scaffolds are inside the ring on top of some sort of bank which the picture does not indicate at all.[3]

A careful reading of the text suggests that the ditch functions within the play in exactly the place where the draughtsman placed it in the original plan—inside the scaffolds, as part of the playing area. If anything, it seems to have functioned to keep the audience out of the 'place'.[4] Absent is the embankment, absent the seated spectators. Nor have any such embankments been found in East Anglia, the probable home of the play. Southern's attractive sketches cannot be depended on, therefore, as an accurate indication of what a medieval production of *The Castle of Perseverance* looked like.

Establishing the character of the touring companies, who produced a different sort of play from those cycles of plays put on annually by the towns and cities of medieval England, most often to celebrate the feast of Corpus Christi, is as difficult as is the task of recreating the conditions under which the civic drama was produced. During the fifteenth century town records begin to include payments to companies of travelling actors. An early example is a payment at Selby Abbey[5] in 1450 to the players of Yorkist lords, but as early as 1385 the records of King's Lynn include payments of half a mark each to players for an 'interlude' (some sort of play; the term is imprecise in medieval usage) on the day of Corpus Christi and for another interlude (apparently on a separate occasion) on that of the martyrdom of St Thomas. Who the actors were, or where they came from, we cannot be sure. Possibly minstrels adapted to the new roles, but most authorities doubt this, considering the survival of minstrels clearly identified as musicians and tellers of tales until late in the fifteenth century. Whoever the actors were, evidence of their activity survives, as well as texts of the plays they produced.[6]

One particular uncertainty with regard to these players arises in connection with a pair of statements found in the 'banns', or summaries of the action, of both *The Castle of Perseverance* and a civic Corpus Christi cycle possibly produced in Lincoln. Both of these plays are long; both are theatrically complicated, requiring elaborate sets and costumes. Both have long parts, requiring considerable dramatic skill. Yet in the banns preceding *The Castle of Perseverance* occurs the following stanza:

> Grace if God wyl graunte us of hys mykyl myth,
> These parcellys in propyrtes we purpose us to playe
> This day seuenenyt before you in syth
> At . . . on the grene in ryal aray.
> Ye haste you thanne thedyrward, syrys, hendly in hyth,
> All goode neyborys ful specyaly we you pray,

---

hendly in hyth graciously and soon

And loke that ye be there betyme, luffely and lyth,
For we schul be onward be vnderne of the day. (ll.131–8)

In the stanza following the scribe has left a blank twice more at similar places in his text, suggesting that the bann-criers were to insert the name of the town where the play was to be put on in the blank spaces. Thus we apparently have a situation where a large, complicated play is being taken on tour, with the bann-criers sent out to outlying towns and villages near to the town chosen for presentation to increase the audience. But the manuscript of the play includes on the last leaf a list of no less than thirty-six actors! As compared with the 'four men and a boy' of the professional touring troupes, or even the nine listed for *The Play of the Sacrament* (another fifteenth-century play) who might play it 'at ease', this is a huge cast. Almost no doubling is possible in the roles written for *The Castle of Perseverance*, yet we know of no companies this large on tour.[7] In fact, we really know very little about fifteenth-century touring companies at all!

If the thought of a touring company of thirty-six gives one pause, much more so is one stopped by the thought of a complete Corpus Christi cycle on tour. Yet this in fact seems to be what we have. At the conclusion of the banns in the manuscript containing the cycle of plays possibly produced in Lincoln, now usually referred to as the N-Town plays, occurs this final address to the audience:

A sunday next yf that we may
At vj of the belle we gynne oure play
In N. towne wherfore we pray
That god now be youre Spede.[8]

It is now generally agreed that the 'N.' stands here for the Latin *nomen*, 'name', meaning that the bann-criers were to insert the appropriate name of a town at this point. Now while we do have some fairly clear evidence that towns did take their plays on tour to neighbouring towns and villages—the records of New Romney for the fifteenth century include payments to both visiting players and bann-criers from neighbouring towns, for example[9]—nothing in the records suggests anything quite as elaborate as an entire cycle on tour.[10] Yet that seems to be what is indicated. Generally speaking the cycles stayed put, the populace came to see them, and spent considerable sums in the process. At the moment we simply do not know how to view the N-Town cycle as the repertory of a touring company.

vnderne afternoon

One further difficulty presents itself to the student of early English drama who is intent on visualizing the original theatrical setting for the surviving plays. In several of the medieval cities of England—York, Chester, Coventry, and Beverley, for example—short plays within each long cycle were presented on movable stages built on wagon beds referred to in the records as 'pageants'. We shall have occasion to concern ourselves with these structures at some length in Chapter 2. For the moment, however, I should merely like to point out that these structures, on which much of the surviving drama was produced, are shadowy shapes indeed. We possess one seventeenth-century description, based on late sixteenth-century notes. Its accuracy is much in doubt. We possess considerable detailed information on the building materials used in their construction, as well as their cost. But as to dimensions, general configuration, or employment in particular theatrical circumstances, we really know very little. For example, Glynne Wickham, in his admirable study of medieval theatrical structures, devotes only six pages out of over 400 to possible reconstruction of the form of the pageant wagons.[11] Most probably the reason for this lies in the fact that whereas elsewhere his account of the forms of fixed theatrical structures is based solidly on documentary evidence, here the neatly-drawn diagram of how the pageants appeared is almost entirely conjecture.

Wickham proposed that a pageant wagon bearing the superstructure that was indubitably necessary for the raising and lowering of heavenly figures by means of windlasses, or the elevated temples, hills, or Heavens called for in numerous stage directions, would be impossibly restricted in its playing area. He also felt that the sight lines would be so obstructed that much of the audience would be unable to see the plays. He therefore proposed, on the basis of some guild payments for scaffolds in the accounts of Coventry, that the York plays were presented on two carts, one, the 'pageant cart', bearing the scenery and superstructure as necessary, the other, the 'scaffold cart', placed in front of the elaborately decorated cart, providing an apron stage. 'A cart of this kind at least corresponds to the booth-theatres of fair grounds depicted in several sixteenth-century paintings and drawings.'[12]

So it does. But there is little evidence to suggest that such a stage was used on the streets of York. In fact there is considerable reason to believe that 'scaffold carts' would have been an impossibility, at least at York. There the locations of performances are known, and can still be seen in much the same form as they appeared in fifteenth-century

York. In Micklegate, whose very name 'Great Street' implies that it was one of the largest in medieval York, the entire space for wagons and audience was not more than thirty-five feet wide.[13] Overhanging buildings built out over the street further restricted the available space. Furthermore the records give no indication that performances were restricted to the wider streets.[14] No matter how narrow one imagines the wagons to have been (a width of ten feet seems a good working hypothesis), it is clear that two placed side-by-side would force virtually all the street audience to view the plays from the sides, an undesirable vantage point.[15] What we have in Wickham's reconstruction, as in Southern's, is a case of a practical man of the modern theatre attempting to reconstruct the conditions of medieval production which he would have liked to have had to produce the particular plays in question. The stages produced are certainly interesting, but in all probability do not represent what the medieval producers of the plays themselves used.

Those who have read C. Walter Hodges' judicious attempt to reconstruct the Globe Theatre in *The Globe Restored* will recognize a familiar situation. Much we know, but often that which we want most to know about the past eludes us. But as with Shakespeare's Globe, the shadowy outlines of the medieval stages need not prevent us from determining where the strengths and weaknesses of the surviving medieval English drama lie; what are its conventions; and, where possible, how the theatrical setting, insofar as we can reconstruct it, determined the form that that drama took. Efforts to dispel the shadows of the past undertaken during the past twenty years of intensive study of England's medieval drama have served only to increase our respect for that drama. In 1945, E. K. Chambers, returning at the end of his life to the field he had done so much to chart originally, stated: 'It is difficult to arrive at any very clear estimate of the literary value of plays which were never intended to be read, and cannot be given life by gestures and intonation of the actors.'[16] In the face of such a magisterial statement of dismissal, one realizes how much courage it took for E. Martin Browne to persuade the sponsors of the Festival of Britain to allow him to produce the York cycle six years later.

One reason why earlier critics of this drama have had such difficulty in assessing its strengths and weaknesses has been the choice of critical criteria. Chambers' yardstick for measuring the literary quality of the York plays, for example, was the study of metrics.[17] In this he was not alone. With the exception of A. C. Cawley's edition of *The*

Wakefield Pageants in the Towneley Cycle, published in 1958, all editions of medieval drama, including the editions of *The Macro Plays* and *Non-Cycle Plays and Fragments* published by the Early English Text Society as recently as 1969 and 1970 respectively, have included lengthy analyses of stanzaic patterns in their introductions. Yet, as Arnold Williams has pointed out, 'Possibly no element in the cycles has been more intensively studied than the versification, especially stanza form. . . . Nearly eighty years of intensive study of certain elements of versification has produced some work important for the critical judgment of the poetic achievements of the cycles—some but not much'.[18] In fact the poetic achievements themselves, whatever their merits, are not the only yardstick to use. Williams' own approach, to which this study will continue to be indebted, is to concentrate instead on the plays as effective theatre, examining them in terms of the traditions of the medieval theatre: that they are worthy of our serious attention will become increasingly clear as our study progresses.[19]

Granting, then, that much must remain uncertain in any discussion of the earliest English drama, let us start by establishing the texts of the surviving plays as firmly as possible in their appropriate locales, and determining as accurately as possible at what point in time they came into being. Once this has been accomplished it will be time to focus on the texts themselves.

We shall begin by establishing the dates of the plays in which the greatest interest has been shown, the four complete cycles of Corpus Christi civic drama. All our surviving dramatic texts of these plays are to be dated at least in the fifteenth century, if not later. To be sure a single date cannot be established for texts as complicated as the surviving manuscripts of the Corpus Christi plays, which are all copies of copies of the plays.

The manuscript of the N-Town cycle, for example, contains the date 1468. The date is in the hand of the scribe responsible for transcribing the bulk of the manuscript. However, it appears at the end of a play on the Purification which represents a third stage of revision in the group of plays in this manuscript which deal with the life of the Virgin.[20] The date is at best a *terminus ad quem*, therefore; but it does establish that the text as we have it contains a composite cycle from the last half of the fifteenth century. The matter of location we will return to later.

In 1885 Lucy Toulmin Smith dated the manuscript of the York plays, both on internal evidence and on the basis of the handwriting, as between 1430 and 1450.[21] Seventy years later Arthur Cawley, in his edition of *The Wakefield Pageants in the Towneley Cycle*, while discussing the matter of influence between the two cycles, could arrive at no more precise date than 1400–50 for that portion of the Towneley cycle derived in part from York. These plays apparently represent the final important revision in the cycle. Some evidence suggests that the latter part of the range is preferable, yet Cawley's conclusion remains, 'While the weight of evidence is therefore in favour of the years 1400–50, there is no strong evidence for preferring one particular decade to another'.[22]

Five of the plays in the Towneley manuscript (this title derives from the name of a previous owner) were borrowed from the York cycle, apparently at a stage in the development of the cycle prior to the state represented by the register edited by Smith. If so, the work of the Wakefield Master in the Towneley manuscript and that of the so-called York Realist, which represents the final stage of revision in the York manuscript, are roughly contemporary. Both are mid-fifteenth-century writers.

The fourth and final cycle for which we have a complete text is much the most important in respect to dates. Five copies of the complete Chester cycle survive, together with a single copy of the play of the *Coming of Antichrist*. The earliest of the five complete copies is dated 1591, the latest 1607. Only the single play, probably of the guild of the Dyers, can be dated as early as *c.* 1500. W. W. Greg, who studied the relationships between the six manuscripts with considerable care, posited hesitantly that 'the common ancestor of P [the single play] and the cyclic manuscripts may well be as early as 1400', but had to admit in a footnote that were a difficult reading at the head of manuscript P to be other than he had proposed, the textual tradition would hardly go back so far.[23] F. M. Salter, working on the metrical structure of the surviving banns, posited an hypothetical 'early' set of banns, containing eighteen plays dating from about 1467. The surviving early Banns of 1540 list twenty-six plays; the late Banns of 1575, when the plays were finally being put down by Protestant ecclesiastical authorities, list twenty-four, the number in the surviving manuscripts. Salter thus states that 'the cycle saw its golden days in the period of Henry VII and Henry VIII when some stability came to England after the long misery of the Wars of the Roses', putting the actual text of the plays among the latest of the four great cycles.[24]

This is hardly the time span upon which histories of medieval

English drama normally focus. Hardin Craig, in his chapter on 'Medieval Religious Drama in England, the Medieval Stage', which prefaces his discussion of the cycle plays, gives what may stand as a typical history of the development of the Corpus Christi cycle plays.

We may believe, then, that the Corpus Christi play was set up, probably on the model of an inclusive dramatic form invented on the Continent, about the end of the first quarter of the fourteenth century at some place probably in the north of England, and spread thence to other places in the island. The play was recognized as a dramatic species in cosmic form; it had one principal geographical location in England; it was uniformly connected with craft guilds or crafts; it was completely established during the fourteenth century, so that by the end of that century the play had become an ancient custom, although there are evidences that the original parts of the play were as yet uncombined in the thirteenth century. There is also evidence that the establishment of the Corpus Christi play was a conscious and deliberate community act.[25]

These articles of faith, which have for some time been offered for our belief, have important consequences in the criticism of the surviving medieval English drama. For one thing, the focus of attention in such a history of the drama is on the period for which no texts survive. Thus Chambers, using for evaluation the metrical yardstick that we have already referred to, stated that 'the texts of such plays as survive have come down to us in a very corrupt state'.[26] Corrupt because the metrics were irregular, not because the characterization was poor, or the handling of the theatrical setting botched.

From such a critical stance has arisen the habit of attempting to reconstruct earlier versions of the surviving cycles rather than concentrating on the qualities of the texts that have survived. An instructive instance of scholarship focussing on states of existence prior to the date of the surviving text is provided by W. W. Greg. He described what he took to be three layers of work in the York cycle, the oldest belonging 'to a simple didactic cycle carefully composed in elaborate stanzas and withal rather dull' (that cycle having largely disappeared, of course), the second not so dull, containing within it as a 'chief distinction . . . such attempts at humour as the collection has to offer' (humour or its absence being another critical yardstick often used to evaluate the early plays). This second layer Greg liked better, too, because it was marked by the work of 'the only great metrist who devoted his talents to the English religious drama as we know it'. Finally, there is the work of the last period, comprising most of the Passion sequence. Greg found this writer 'a very remarkable though uneven writer. A

metrist he certainly is not; he writes in powerful but loose and rugged
alliterative verse. He also writes at great length and with much rhetoric
and rant. But he is a real dramatist, and his portrait of Pilate is mas-
terly'.[27] Greg dated the work of this last writer 'hardly earlier than
1400'; the clear effect of this dating is to suggest that the cycle as trans-
cribed in the register was already of some age by the mid-fifteenth
century, all three hypothetical cycles having been composed by 1400.
Reconstructing the three cycles rather than interpreting the one that
survives, and assessing the hypothetical works so reconstructed by such
criteria as metrical regularity and the presence of comic realism, are
the critical tasks Greg set himself.

   The consequence of such criticism could have been predicted. A. P.
Rossiter, who found the cycle drama interesting only when it portrayed the 'devilish as the inversion, reversal, or parody of the divine',[28]
scored the critical habit of searching out what he called the 'geologic
"intrusions" of varying date and intention' as further complicating
the criticism of a drama 'crude and, in the older strata, insipid to a
degree beyond *Hymns Ancient and Modern* at its tritest'. Greg's three
layers in the York cycle are then summarized as a signal case in point
of what we might call the 'geological' school of criticism.[29]

   Whether or not the plays are 'crude' or 'insipid'—and there is a
growing body of criticism which suggests that they are far otherwise—
continual efforts to establish what they are not but once might have been
will not help us to understand their merits. But there is another cogent
reason for distrusting in large part histories of the medieval English
drama which focus on the purported events of the fourteenth century.
Most of the evidence upon which the hypothetical sequence of development is based has proven to be shaky indeed. To begin with, the
setting up of cycles in the first quarter of the fourteenth century has
proven to be far out as to date. The crucial piece of evidence for such
a statement is the supposed date of 1327 for the beginnings of English
vernacular drama in Chester. Since the festival of Corpus Christi was
officially promulgated in 1311, the Chester date seemed to provide the
necessary progression in the supposed turn of events. However, the
date of 1327 arose apparently from Chambers' attempt to manage
an inaccurate description of the contents of William Newhall's 1532
Proclamation for the Chester plays. Of the three different authors'
names proposed by the Proclamation as fathering the cycle—Sir (a
common title for a priest in this period) John Arneway, Sir Henry
Francis, and Ranulph Higden—only Sir Henry Francis appears as a

likely parent. He was abbot of St Werburgh's Abbey, where the cycle traditionally commenced playing until its demise. While abbot he signed two charters dated 1377 and 1382.[30] As F. M. Salter remarked, 'the moment we accept the possibility that the Plays were initiated by Sir Henry Francis, we find that they come into being at the very time when we have our earliest references to mystery plays elsewhere, for the earliest firm references to English mystery plays are those to York in 1376, Beverley in 1377, London in 1378, and Coventry in 1392'.[31] And even those late dates may not refer to fully developed cyclic plays of the type which have survived.[32]

We certainly have single vernacular plays early in the fourteenth century. The manuscript for *Dux Moraud*, a speaker's part for a play on the tale of the incestuous daughter, is generally dated on linguistic grounds 1300–25; the fragmentary *Interludium de Clerico et Puella*, possibly an early farce, dates from the same period. As already noted, an interlude was performed at King's Lynn on Corpus Christi day in 1385 by travelling players. Their reward was half a mark. In the same year the townsfolk of Lynn also saw a play of St Thomas Martyr, for which the reward was also half a mark. As these were paid for by a town's governing body, and were put on by itinerant players, it is unlikely that they were in Latin. However, no part of the cycle plays which have survived was written before the very last part of the fourteenth century.[33] Composites they may be, but composites formed in the literary *milieu* of the fifteenth century. As such they are contemporary with the surviving moralities, whose traditional dating as productions of the fifteenth and sixteenth centuries has been recently reaffirmed by modern editors. The earliest of these, *The Pride of Life* and *The Castle of Perseverance*, both dated *c.* 1425, should be considered as appearing at roughly the same time as the surviving texts of cycle plays came into being. Theatrical practices and traditions, thematic concerns, indeed, all aspects of the early drama, should be seen as developing simultaneously, with the borrowings and influences taking place more often within self-contained geographical areas than within literary *genres* constructed after the fact. Most of the forms of dramatic activity found in England in the fifteenth and sixteenth centuries had been developed on the continent by the end of the thirteenth century, it is true, though the English dramatists need not have drawn on that tradition at the same time that romances were being translated for English audiences in the late fourteenth century. Our concern must in any case be to concentrate on what was made of the inherited continental dramatic tradition, rather than to attempt reconstructions of prior states of existence.

Since influences within geographical areas are important, and since practices vary from the North to the East Midlands to the South, it is well to review what is known as to the location of the surviving dramas without for the moment discussing the evidence. Taking first the major Corpus Christi cycles, those of York and Chester can be placed with no difficulty. They have always been associated with the place-names they are known by, as can the surviving portions of the Coventry cycle. The Towneley manuscript is generally regarded as coming entirely from the town of Wakefield, though many are still hesitant to call the entire cycle 'the Wakefield cycle'. As already noted, the original home of the fourth cycle is in some doubt. The state of the manuscript corresponds well with the sequence of events in Lincoln insofar as it is possible to reconstruct them.[34] However, there are undeniable points of similarity between the language of the main scribe and the language of East Anglia, especially Norfolk.[35] At the moment we know of no centre in the Norfolk area sufficiently active in drama to have undertaken so ambitious a cycle. For the time being we are at least safe in placing the cycle on the eastern edge of the East Midlands.

When we turn to the surviving non-cyclic drama, that is, of separate plays, we find that the majority also derive from the same area. Let us take the plays in the Macro manuscript, *The Castle of Perseverance*, *Wisdom*, and *Mankind*. The most recent editor of these plays has concluded that 'The manuscript of *The Castle* could not have been written by a scribe from Lincolnshire, but it may very well have been written by a scribe from Norfolk'.[36] Despite an internal reference in the play to the gallows of Canwick outside the city of Lincoln, therefore, a Norfolk origin for this play seems to be indicated. The language of *Wisdom* is also close to that of Norfolk or Suffolk, and is certainly East Anglian.[37] Finally, internal references to places in Cambridge-shire, Norfolk, and Bury support the East Anglian dialect of *Mankind*, to place it in the same general area as *Wisdom*.

The *Non-Cycle Plays and Fragments* originally collected for the Early English Text Society by Osborn Waterhouse in 1909 have recently been re-edited by Norman Davis. Several of the plays included in this volume derive from East Anglia, including not only the Norwich Grocers' play on the Fall, but also the separate play of *Abraham and Isaac* from Brome Hall in Suffolk (the apparent area in which the play was written) and *The Play of the Sacrament*, which apparently comes from Thetford in Norfolk.[38] In addition there are dramatic extracts from a Norfolk commonplace book, and a dramatic fragment in Anglo-Norman and English from the manor of Rickingshall in Suffolk, a possession of the Abbey at Bury St Edmunds, as well as the speaker's part *Dux Moraud* already alluded to. Of this Davis states that 'The strongly East Anglian character of the language of the play is consonant with the Norfolk-Suffolk origin of the parchment roll on which it is written'.[39] The dramatic prologue found in Cambridge University Library resembles in its language that of *The Pride of Life*, however, which Davis would place in Ireland. The remainder of the pieces collected are from a variety of locations—parts for an actor in a group of liturgical plays from Shrewsbury, an Abraham and Isaac play from Northampton, a Noah play from Newcastle, a prologue to a miracle of the Virgin from Durham, and finally an unlocalized fragment from a manuscript in the Bodleian library. Altogether six of the thirteen pieces are East Anglian in origin, the remainder being of miscellaneous origin.

There remains one other important group of fifteenth-century English plays, the collection known as Digby 133. The titles of the 'Digby plays' as they appear in Furnivall's edition are *Herod's Killing of the Children*, *The Conversion of St Paul*, *Mary Magdalene*, and an imperfect copy of *Wisdom*. Furnivall added two plays on *Christ's Burial and Resurrection* from Bodleian MS E Museo 160. In the course of preparing an edition of these last two plays, which bear no relation to the others, D. C. Baker and J. L. Murphy have concluded that the so-called Digby plays all date from the first turn of the sixteenth century, and that though 'all vary considerably in dialect . . . that is not vital: the language of all four is consonant generally with an East Midland origin'.[40] Other than a fragmentary Robin Hood play from Norfolk, and the Cornish *Ordinalia*, some plays by Medwall, and the best-known medieval play, *The Summoning of Everyman*, this comprises the corpus of medieval English drama.

From such a survey it is clear that a large proportion of the surviving drama is from the East Midlands. Virtually all of it is distinctively different both in content and theatrical practice from the surviving Corpus Christi drama of York, Chester, Wakefield, and Coventry, for the East Midlands appear to have relied much more heavily on the place-and-scaffold method of staging so popular on the continent than did the cities of the West Midlands and the North. In order to approach the dramatic qualities of the plays which are likely to interest the modern audience, it will be necessary to establish the nature of the theatrical conventions first of the East Midlands and then of the North. Once these two major traditions are understood, and their possibilities explored, it will then be appropriate to suggest how one might approach English medieval drama on its own terms.

Rather than attempting a survey of all the surviving plays, it will be our task to establish model critical approaches to the plays which both accept their differences from the drama of the succeeding ages, with the changes in conventions that ensue with the changing theatres of England, and which at the same time stress their dramatic qualities independent of time and place. For in the last analysis fine plays always succeed for the same reasons, no matter in what age they are written. Instead of the study of metrics, the analysis of successive geological strata within the cycles, or scouting for comic touches, we shall concentrate on the actual conventions employed by the medieval dramatists themselves in order to arrive at an understanding of the appropriate criteria to use in assessing that drama's worth.

2

THE MAJOR THEATRICAL TRADITIONS

A dramatist writing civic drama at the turn of the fifteenth century in England had two well developed theatrical traditions at his disposal. The first had, by the end of the twelfth century, been created on the continent for the complex Latin plays performed in the cathedrals of the High Middle Ages. Such a play is the Beauvais *Play of Daniel*. Noah Greenberg's modernized version has demonstrated the dramatic power of such a play, which relies primarily on music, costuming, and processional movement for its effect between relatively unlocalized playing areas. More ambitious was the Tegernsee *Play of Antichrist*, requiring for its performance many actors and a large stage, with a temple of God and seven royal *sedes*, or raised scaffold stages, together with room for processional marching, counter-marching, and warfare.[1] Latin plays written in this tradition regularly preserved the ceremonial features of their origin.[2]

Related to these plays but lacking the ceremonial qualities, and also from the twelfth century, are the *Jeu d'Adam* and the *Seinte Resurrection*.[3] We have no idea whether these plays exerted any direct influence on the vernacular plays in English which appeared two centuries later. What is certain is that the staging of these two plays anticipates that of later fully-developed mystery cycles both in England and on the continent. Of the two the stage directions of the *Jeu d'Adam* are the most instructive, particularly the opening direction, often quoted, but worth reproducing again here in full.

Paradise shall be set up in a fairly high place; curtains and silk cloths shall be hung around it, at such a height that the persons who shall be in Paradise can be seen from the shoulders upwards. Fragrant flowers and leaves shall be planted there; there shall also be various trees with fruit hanging on them, so that it looks a very pleasant place. Then shall come God the Saviour wearing a dalmatic, and Adam and Eve shall be stationed in front of him. Adam shall wear a red tunic, but Eve a woman's garment in white with a white silk scarf; and they shall both stand in front of God—Adam, however, nearer to God with a calm countenance, Eve with face lowered. Adam shall be well trained not to answer too quickly nor too slowly, when he has to answer. Not only Adam but all the actors shall be instructed to control their speech and to make their actions appropriate to the matter they speak of; and, in speaking the verse, not to add a syllable, nor to take one away, but to enunciate everything distinctly, and to say everything in the order laid down. Whenever anyone shall speak of Paradise, he shall look towards it and point it out with his hand.[4]

Clearly the author of this stage direction had considerable practical theatrical experience. The directions to the actors resemble nothing so much as those Hamlet gave his old friends five hundred years later. Costuming is formal and symbolic: Adam's red garment could betoken such virtues as magnanimity or power, or the age when man is characterized by virility; Eve's white garment is clearly to be associated with innocence and purity.[5] No question of stage nudity here! The symbolic quality of the costuming is underlined when later the dramatist specifies that after Adam has eaten the apple, 'bending so that the onlookers cannot see him, he shall take off his fine clothes and put on poor clothes sewn with figleaves'.[6] Of particular interest is the structure specified for Paradise. It is, to begin with, raised, 'in a higher place'— *loco eminenciori* is the actual expression used—and walled about, as in the medieval illuminations of the garden of Paradise. Again, as in the illuminations, it is the trees and flowers, characterized by the same bright colours used by the illuminators, that the dramatist specifies. All this is to be done 'so that it looks a very pleasant place',[7] certainly in contrast to the other stage structure to be used, namely, Hell Mouth. This is not described in the same detail, for the general features of Hell Mouth as an animalistic structure had become standard. This one must have been of considerable size, for as Adam and Eve are led off in chains at their death, the stage direction reads

some of the devils shall point to them as they come, and shall receive them and despatch them to hell. From hell they shall make a great smoke to arise, and shall shout to each other in their joy; and they shall bang their cauldrons and kettles together so that they can be heard outside.[8]

Returning to the opening stage direction, one further point should be noted. The dramatist specifies that the actors shall come in—'Then shall come God the Savior . . . and Adam and Eve shall be stationed in front of him'—but it is clear from the subsequent action that they do not enter Paradise. Rather, God first addresses them, then points out Paradise, and finally leads them into Paradise from the area where they first appeared, retiring after indicating the forbidden fruit 'into the Church'.[9] The area in which the action first began is then invested by devils. The stage direction reads 'Meanwhile devils shall run about the "places"', (*per plateas*).[10] A great deal of the action takes place in the 'place', much of it characteristically movement from one structure to another, as when Satan goes from Hell to Paradise to tempt Adam and Eve. Other action can occur in the place, however; once ejected from Paradise, Adam and Eve take a spade and mattock and 'begin to cultivate the ground and they shall sow wheat in it', (*et incipiet* [*sic*] *colere terram, et seminabunt in ea triticum*). Having finished this, they are to move off and 'sit somewhere for a little while, as if wearied of work. . . . Meanwhile, the devil shall come and shall plant thorns and thistles in their plot and go away'.[11] The result is that Adam despairs, the two recriminate one another, and finally are led off, manacled, to Hell.

While it is clear from these directions that the actors must be able to move freely through this acting area, one direction indicates that the audience was in close proximity to the actors. After Adam has angrily rejected Satan's second suggestion that he eat the apple, sending him off with splendid outrage, Satan first sulks over to Hell Mouth 'where he shall talk with the other devils. After that he shall run around among the spectators' (*post ea vero discursum faciet per populum*).[12] It is worth noting that since we know from God's exits into the church that the 'place' is unquestionably the open area before the church door, the populace must be standing on the same level as the action in the place. Obviously we do not have an auditorium canted to improve sight lines.

To summarize, then, we find in the *Jeu d'Adam* actors of whom considerable histrionic skill is expected,[13] dressed in elaborate, symbolic clothing of a contemporary cut. These actors move between three separate locations, one a raised stage, one a Hell Mouth of sufficient size to accommodate the entrances and exits of several actors at one time on ground level, and one the church, representing Heaven. As in the tympani over the great west portals of medieval churches and cathedrals, or in the illustrations for later medieval plays reproduced by Allardyce Nicoll,[14] Hell Mouth would have been located stage left. Heaven is normally located at extreme stage right by contrast—it is so placed in Axton and Stevens' diagram of the staging for the *Seinte Resurreccion* [15]—but where the church is being used for Heaven, it is likely that Paradise occupied stage right. Action takes place as often in the 'place' as in the structured locations. The audience is sufficiently close to the 'place' for actors to move easily among them, but probably leaves the central area free of encumbrance.

These are essentially the characteristics of the theatre we now most usually refer to as 'place-and-scaffold'. It is the term I shall use hereafter to describe such a theatre. It is basically the theatre of the *Seinte Resurreccion*, except that the number of scaffolds has been expanded. There the separate locations are referred to both as *maisuns*, 'houses' (one also finds the term 'mansions' used), or *lius*, 'places'. There are seven of the former and eight of the latter. Axton and Stevens note that 'The *C* "prologue" distinguishes between "houses" (*maisuns*), which are structural, and "places" (*lius*), which are merely areas of ground where characters belong, and which may have been marked out with rope or stones'.[16] Because the stage directions in the *Seinte Resurreccion* are less explicit, we cannot visualize as readily the form of the *maisuns*. But for the moment this is of no consequence. What is important to note is that the concept of an acting area flanked by structures, whether raised or on the same level as the *platea* or 'place', representing separate locations necessary to an involved dramatic action extending over considerable time and space, had evolved on the continent by the end of the twelfth century as fully as this theatrical setting was ever to evolve in England. From such illustrations as that for the later Valenciennes mystery play it is clear that the structures used in such theatres need not be realistic.[17] Rather they resemble in their architectural forms the stylized stables familiar in so many medieval Nativity scenes.

Place-and-scaffold staging is the characteristic theatrical setting in France in the Middle Ages, and for much of what we know of the drama of the German-speaking countries as well. The surviving illustrations and schematic diagrams, nearly all from the continent, predominantly illustrate this method of staging. Before discussing the extent to which it prevailed in England, however, we need to review what is known of the other major theatrical tradition also present in England at the turn of the fifteenth century. As I have stated in the first chapter, we know that a number of medieval English cities produced their Corpus Christi cycle plays on wheeled structures of some sort. One difficulty that arises in determining what these structures

were like results from the casual manner in which the common terms
for the structures were handled in the early records. The terms which
appear most frequently in the early records, generally kept in Latin
till well into the fifteenth century, were *pagina* and *pagenda*, and, in the
plural, *pagentes* (the latter two obviously influenced by the vernacular
term 'pageant'). These terms occur most frequently in records of the
events on Corpus Christi day. The problem is best illustrated in the
records of the town of Beverley.

In 1377 the town council ordered the guild of the Tailors in that town
to appear in person at their annual accounting of their expenses for a
pageant of a play of Corpus Christi (*pagine ludi Corporis Christi*). A. F.
Leach, who edited the Beverley documents, translated *pagine* in this
instance as 'stage'.[18] So it may be translated, if one realizes that the
pagina, *pagenda*, or pageant is a rather special sort of stage. An entry
for 1390 requires thirty-eight craft guilds to have their 'plays and
pageants—*ludos et pagentes*—ready henceforth on every Corpus
Christi day, in the fashion and form of the ancient custom of the town
of Beverley, to play in honour of the Body of Christ'.[19] Whether or
not the 'ancient custom' (*antiquam consuetudinem*) stretches much
back beyond 1377 is doubtful. What is of more importance for our
present concerns is the fact that in this entry, as in a number that
follow shortly after, the terms *pagenda* or *pagentes* are carefully kept
separate from the term *ludus*, and that they are clearly meant to refer
to the structure on which the play was performed. In 1411, when the
town council sought to involve 'worshipful men of the worthier
sort' (*reverendis de dignioribus*) who were not guild members to en-
courage them in support of a play, the agreement reached was for
them to construct 'a proper and fit pageant' (*honestam et honorabilem
pagendam*) on which to play 'a proper play' (*honestum ludum*).[20]

But later in the same entry the terminological confusion begins.
Speaking of the craft guilds' involvement in the feast of Corpus
Christi, the council ordered that annually forever they should play
their pageants of the play of Corpus Christi as they were wont to do
(*annuatim imperpetuum ludant pagendas ludi Corporis Christi quas ludere
consueverunt*). Leach translated *pagendas* here as 'scenes', rather than his
more usual 'stage' or 'pageant', indicating his own uncertainty as to
the meaning of the term in this context.[21] In 1414, when the council
reviewed the constitution of the craft of Barbers, it is recorded as
providing that they shall 'annually forever play or caused to be played
a certain pageant' (*ludant vel ludifaciant quamdam pagendam*) representing

St John baptizing Christ in the river Jordan and that they shall play at
such time as the community agrees that the 'plays shall be played'
(*pagendas ludi*)[22]. Here the term is clearly synonymous with *ludus*,
'play'. In 1493 the constitution of the Drapers' guild called for them
'to play or cause to be played at the feast of Corpus Christi a certain
pageant called Demyng Pylate' (*ludant vel ludi faciant in Festo Corporis
Christi quamdam pagendam vocatam Demyng Pylate*).[23] The pageant
'Demyng Pylate' must refer to the entire dramatic production rather
than solely to the structure on which the play was presented. Thus
when at Hereford in 1501 we find a list of twenty-seven 'paiants for the
procession of Corpus Christi' assigned to different crafts, we cannot
be certain what is meant, though by this time it is probable that plays,
not wagons, are intended.[24] The meaning is most probably that of the
banns to the N-Town cycle, where each separate play within the cycle
is called a pageant.

What I have described is a normal semantic development, where a
term's original meaning is extended to operations associated with the
object originally signified by the term. When the term first appears,
in the latter portion of the fourteenth century, it refers to the wheeled
stage structures associated with the dramatic productions presented
with the Corpus Christi procession held on that feast day. By the end
of the fifteenth century certainly, and probably earlier in the fifteenth
century as well, though when we cannot be certain, it refers both to the
vehicles and the plays produced in this theatrical setting. We cannot
deduce from early uses of the term that when a writer speaks of a
pageant he necessarily is talking about a dramatic performance. He
may be talking about what we now call a 'float'—an elaborate set
containing a *tableau vivant*. For example, the *Ordo paginarum ludi
Corporis Christi* entered in the York Memorandum Book by the town
clerk, Roger Burton, in 1415 is more likely to be a description of the
pageant wagons than of the plays themselves. In medieval France where
the wheeled stages were used, drawn along a line of march while the
audience remained stationary, as at Béthune, Abbéville or Lille, the
performances were more usually dumb shows than true plays. Such a
presentation took place in Paris in 1313, in honour of the visit of Edward
II of England and his wife, Isabelle of France. The chroniclers of the
event reported that the entire life of Christ from birth to resurrection
was presented, that at least ninety angels and over one hundred devils
took part, and that, in addition to diverse spectacles portraying the life
of the blessed and the damned, there were also scenes from the cycle

of Renard the Fox! According to Grace Frank, such *mystères mimés* were usually presented at great festivals, or on the occasion of royal entries.[25]

The idea that the first plays written to be performed on the wheeled stages developed from *tableaux vivants* rather than from the liturgical Latin plays, and therefore stem from a different set of theatrical traditions, is not by any means a new one. As early as 1892 Charles Davidson proposed such an idea in his *Studies in the Early Mystery Plays*.[26] Chambers as well, in his chapter on 'Moralities, Puppet-plays, Pageants', cited numerous examples of tableaux presented on pageant wagon stages, not the least of which are a group of tableaux for which John Lydgate wrote a set of descriptive verses entitled 'Ordenaunce of a processyon of the fest of Corpus Christi, made in London by Daun John Lydegate'.[27] But representations of purely visual scenes in Corpus Christi processions were not accepted as a possibility since such occurrences did not square with the theory of the organic growth of the early cycles from liturgical plays.[28] Because they believed in the gradual passage of the plays from their liturgical origins into secular control as they moved from the control of the clergy to that of the laity, scholars such as Chambers or Hardin Craig strained hard, as we have seen, to construct a hypothetical sequence of events in the fourteenth century in which early Corpus Christi cycle plays were supposed to have been performed at such places as Chester and Cambridge. But if the dates we have established earlier are more nearly correct, there is no direct line of organic growth from twelfth-century liturgical Latin plays to the plays written for pageant wagon stages at the close of the fourteenth century. Rather there is every reason to follow instead the suggestion of V. A. Kolve that the particular subjects and the order in which they appear in an English cycle of Corpus Christi plays were deliberately selected to play the history of the world, from Creation to Judgment, in which the life of Christ is the central event.[29] There is no reason at all why the representation of the important events in this sequence should not have been purely visual at first, or have involved speeches not much longer than those prepared by Lydgate.

If one regards the early pageant stages as but one part of the elaborate pageantry in use for all sorts of state and festive occasions not only in France but in England as well, one realizes immediately how closely allied these theatres are to the structures described so fully by Glynne Wickham. Before attempting to reconstruct the pageant wagon as a set, therefore, let us note some of the characteristics of the static pageant sets.[30] The most usual event which called for the erection of pageant stages in the street was a royal entry. To ensure stability, and reduce the need for sturdy framing, permanent architectural features of the streets, such as market crosses, conduits, and city gates, were utilized for the structures erected. Wickham distinguishes sharply between the pageant stages, which suggest 'at least a special occasion and a spectacular display quite out of the ordinary', and the familiar booth stages used by 'mountebanks, professional minstrels or players on public holidays or at other times of regular general assembly'.[31] The latter, raised on barrels or trestles with a curtained enclosure at the rear for quick changes, is the stage of the interlude, a thing of the day, to be struck as a circus is struck today, vanishing once the occasion is over.[32] Because the morality and the interlude, the stock-in-trade of the touring players, were long thought to be the dominant influence on the early Elizabethan theatres, those stages were long viewed as being bare and unadorned as the booth stages themselves. Wickham's concern, therefore, has been to underline the continuing life of what is in many ways an even sturdier theatrical tradition, the tradition of the pageant stages, sturdier because it was so widespread, and involved so many people in its construction and maintenance.

To begin with, pageant stages were apparently from a very early date associated with processions. Wickham cites a number of thirteenth-century royal entries into London in which elaborate paraphernalia were prepared for the triumphal procession. The procession celebrating Edward I's defeat of the Scots at Falkirk in 1298 is particularly notable in that some of the pageantry was provided by craft guilds. Unlike the equally elaborate tournaments, with their lists and scaffolds for spectators, which were an activity of the nobility, the street pageants 'were essentially bourgeois activities, responsibility for their devising and enactment lying with the municipality in liaison with the ecclesiastical authorities'.[33] This, of course, is the administrative arrangement which prevailed throughout the life of the Corpus Christi plays, which never ceased being a regular part of the religious life of the towns. One can see this most clearly in the arrangements made for the visit of Queen Margaret to Coventry in 1456. Just as with the Corpus Christi procession, the town council took it in hand to organize the first order of business, the financing of the gift and shows. Then followed in the Coventry *Leet Book* a memorandum on the order of shows for Queen Margaret's entry. Taking the order printed in Appendix III of *Two Coventry Corpus Christi Plays* as edited by Hardin Craig together with the eighteenth-century map of the city from Bradford's survey that Craig includes as a frontispiece, one can easily see how such a procession was handled.[34]

The procession entered Coventry from the west at Bablake Gate, on the extreme left of Bradford's map. There the city fathers erected 'a Jesse [tree?] over the yate'. Elaborate trees had become a staple of medieval stage craft at least from the twelfth century, as we have seen in the *Jeu d'Adam*. Jesse trees appear frequently in medieval stained glass; there also is a Jesse play in the N-Town cycle. In such windows as the great Jesse window in St Mary's Church, Shrewsbury, the scheme is not necessarily purely genealogical, but as in the N-Town cycle version, can include both the kings in the line of Jesse and the prophets, both of whom glorify the Incarnation as well as the Blessed Virgin, often enthroned at the summit of the window.[35] Not all the figures in the window have individual prophecies, some simply echoing the words of others in the window. One can therefore see what sort of visual impact a fully developed Jesse tree would have, with a figure of the Virgin at its top, in which two of the Prophets make the specific equation between Queen Margaret and the Virgin, Jeremiah even likening her directly to 'the rote of Jesse rote'.[36]

The procession then moved a short way along Smith Street to the square before St John's Church. Before the gate at the east end of the church 'was a pagent right well arayed and therein was shewed a speche of seynt Edward and an-other of seynt John the Euangelist'. We have no way of reconstructing this stage, called quite clearly a 'pageant', nor the one which followed, built around the conduit to the east in Smithford Street, containing the 'iiij cardynall vertues', all of whom deliver short speeches. Clearly there was an elaborate structure at the next station, built around the large cross in Cross Cheaping, for the memorandum here reads 'there were ordeyned diverse angels sensyng a-high on the cross, and there ranne out wyne at mony places a long while'. This pageant must have been of the 'No expense has been spared' variety. There then followed, at the wide end of Cross Cheaping Street, between the cross and the conduit, as the direction notes, 'ix pagentes right well arayed and yn every pagent was shewed a speche of the ix conqueroures'. Craig thought that because a pageant was specified at St John's Church, and nine for the nine worthies were specified in Cross Cheaping, that the ten pageants he had posited for the Corpus Christi plays were in fact used here, particularly because 'in the *Leet Book* "pageant" means the vehicle on which the plays were acted'.[37]

We have already observed that early usage of the term refers to the structure rather than the play, but it is not correct to say further that the structure indicated is always and in every case wheeled. It would certainly strengthen the case for close connections between the stages constructed for royal entries and those for religious processions to be able to state that Coventry's pageant wagons were rolled out for this occasion. But I doubt it. What distinguishes the pageants referred to in this procession from the stages otherwise described is that the structures for the Jesse tree, for St John and St Edward, the four Cardinal Virtues, and the censing angels, as for the final structure built around the conduit in Cross Cheaping, containing 'as mony virgyns as might be ther-uppon' as well as 'a grete dragon and St Margaret sleyng hym be myracull'—all are built around permanent architectural features. The rest have their own, 'pageant', stages.

I have not cited in full the stages for this mid-fifteenth-century royal entry because the memorandum describing them is readily available for consultation in Craig's edition. Wickham makes it clear that the structures there described are all similar to structures built in England in the latter part of the fourteenth century. One in parti-cular I would like to quote in full as it demonstrates as well as any of the material he has collected just how elaborate these structures can be. The description, taken from Walsingham's *Historia Anglicana*, is of one of the stages built for the procession celebrating Richard II's coronation in 1377. Wickham's translation of the Latin description in Walsingham's *Historia Anglicana* is as follows:

Nor did these great guilds [in the procession] lack a large company of flutes and trumpets: for every guild (*in the procession*) is led by its own trumpeters. Trumpeters had been stationed by the Londoners above the Conduit, as above the tower in the same street, which had been built in the King's honour, to sound a fanfare on his approach. . . . For a kind of castle had been constructed having four towers, in the upper part of the shopping street called Cheapside: and from two of its sides wine flowed abundantly. In its towers, moreover, four very beautiful maidens had been placed, of about the King's own age and stature and dressed in white garments. There was one in each of the four towers. On the King's approach being sighted, they scattered golden leaves in his path, and, on his coming nearer, they showered imitation gold florins onto both him and his horse. When he had arrived in front of the castle, they took gold cups and, filling them with wine at the spouts of the said castle, offered them to him and his retinue. In the top of the castle, and raised above and be-tween its four towers, a golden angel had been devised with such cunning that, on the King's arrival, it bent down and offered him the crown.[38]

While it is not certain from the Latin wording, Wickham believes, from the evidence of the spouting wine, and other later structures built around the Great Conduit, that this castle was built on and around the conduit, as were the later structures at Coventry. However they were built, they certainly employed sophisticated engineering features in their design. When one remembers that these were coupled with bright colours and rich costuming for the actors, one realizes that these structures were indeed impressive. And all of this array of machinery and elaborate superstructure was known to and used by the makers of the movable pageant stages.

But it is one thing to build an elaborate elevated structure with the internal gears and windlasses for operating clockwork figures, as well as operating plumbing to pour forth an abundance of wine, and another to put such gear onto a structure that can be wheeled about the narrow streets of a medieval city such as York. Nor, when we come to visualize the early pageant wagons as opposed to the fixed pageant stages, are we helped by the nature of the surviving evidence. To begin with, all the scraps of surviving evidence are late. As already noted, the one verbal description of a wagon stage which survives is possibly from as late a date as the early seventeenth century—hardly a firm basis for reconstruction. The account is by one David Rogers, the son of Archdeacon Robert Rogers, the author of the *Breviarye* of Chester history. F. M. Salter seriously questioned the reliability of Rogers' account, on which many of the reconstructed wheeled pageant stages have been based.[39] Yet it appears that David Rogers was in fact using his father's manuscript notes, which date from the last years of the Chester cycle.[40] Rogers' account is thus still late—late sixteenth-century—but it may very well be accurate. Since the surviving account books for the details of production strongly suggest that once developed, the wagon stages remained essentially the same throughout the period of their use, it seems worth reproducing Rogers' account:

these pagiantes or cariage was a highe place made like ahowse with ij rowmes beinge open on the tope the lower rowme they apparrelled & dressed them selues, and in the higher rowme they played, and they stoode vpon 6 wheeles And when they had done with one cariage in one place they wheeled the same from one streete to an other. . . .[41]

The rest of Rogers' account describes how the wagons were wheeled from station to station in succession during the three days of production, without stopping.

This account may not be far out. There are records of a number of
payments for pageant cloths, apparently to cover the wheels from view.
For example, in 1440 the Coventry Smiths paid 3s 4d for 'cloth to lap
abowt the pajent [of the Passion] payntyng and all'.[42] Certainly this
practice is commonly used for modern floats. Once such a system had
developed it does seem reasonable to suppose that the method of
providing access to the enclosed space below through a trap would
evolve to provide for appearances, disappearances, and costume
changes which otherwise would be impossible. If the action is, however, not much beyond that of a *tableau vivant*, such effects would not
be required. I am inclined to believe that the early wagons did not
require elaborate action, and that we should therefore regard this part
of Rogers' description as a late development. Secondly, there is the
matter of the 'open room' above. Surviving paintings of Baroque
pageant stages for *tableaux vivants* at Louvain (1594) and Brussels
(1615) more often than not show roofed structures, and references to
pillars for holding up coverings to these stages support this evidence.
Rogers has been attacked on this point, therefore.[43] But if he meant
simply that the lower part of the wagon was enclosed on all four sides,
but that the upper part, roofed or not, was open to all four sides, I
suggest that this description is not a bad one.[44]

The general size can only be guessed at. Salter collected much information on the sums paid for the houses where the wagons were
stored from year to year between performances. Annual rents varied
mostly between 4d and 8d. At the close of the period when the plays
were being produced, in 1574, the Coopers received 5s 4d each from
the Painters and the Skinners who rented their pageant on the second
and third days of the performance. Of the attempts at converting these
sums to modern equivalents which Salter makes (a notoriously difficult task, and not even equivalent to modern figures after twenty
years of continuous inflation!), probably the most successful is that
which equates the penny to a day's wage of eight to nine dollars a day
for rough labour in Edmonton, Alberta in June of 1954. This yielded a
modern equivalent of $500 rent for that one day's use, and around $70
a year for garaging. The structure *has* to have been fully as elaborate as
the late fourteenth-century stationary pageant stages already described.
Arnold Williams, using the figures in the paintings of the Brussels
'triumph' for scale, computed that the overall dimensions of the stage
itself could not exceed eight feet by twenty feet.[45] Considering the
dimensions of the streets in York, which varied between twenty-five

and thirty feet, these dimensions do seem to be the maximum we can use. Furthermore, since the wagons had to be drawn from place to place by from seven to ten men, even if the streets were wider, considerations of weight would certainly have imposed a limit on the size of the movable stages.

On these structures were built the altars for Cain and Abel, the Nativity mangers, crosses, sepulchres, and Hell Mouths. Such structures occupy space, as they do in pictures of continental pageant carts. Salter reckoned that the Chester Shepherds' Play required 'a mound at one side of the stage, a stable at the other, a moving star, and an appearing and disappearing angel'.[46] The Coventry Drapers, who put on the play of the Last Judgment, in one year paid for the following properties: 'Hell-mouth—a fire kept at it; windlass and three fathom of cord; earthquake, barrell for the same, a pillar for the words of the barrell painted; three worlds painted and a piece that bears them; a link to set the world on fire; pulpits for the angels; cross, rosin, a ladder.'[47] The burning worlds must have been quite separate from the structure bearing the pulpits and Hell-mouth. Access to the world must have been via the ladder leading from the pageant stage to a separate part of the acting area. Nevertheless, the pageant stage would be full. Not only would the sets have contained such three-dimensional structures; the plays often have fairly large casts. The maximum number of actors on a wagon at one time in the York cycle was twenty-six in the Triumphal Entry into Jerusalem; including the children referred to in the play, there may have been as many as thirty. Here the solution offered by M. James Young makes excellent sense; since the main action of the play is Christ's passage on an ass, it seems probable that the pageant wagon represented a small castle where the ass is secured, a tree for Zaccheus to climb, and possibly a simple representation of the gate of the city, with most of the action taking place in the street.[48] Otherwise the Last Judgment has seventeen, with a number of other plays requiring from twelve to fifteen on the wagon at once. 'Here, as in the disciple plays [where one must accommodate a group of thirteen in addition to the other actors], in religious art, and in the *tableaux vivants*, a great many people can be accommodated in a small space if they are treated as a group and not individualized.'[49] Static groups do fill up the stage, nevertheless. But we must remember that if the static pageant stages built around permanent features of the street provided small opportunity for stage action, the *tableaux vivants* provided even less. The theatrical conventions of these movable pageant stages must clearly differ from the conventions of the place-and-scaffold theatres, and must be used when reading plays written for such stages.

It remains to indicate how these movable pageant stages were characteristically employed. From the earliest records on they are associated with the Corpus Christi procession. The earliest reference, from Beverley in 1377, refers to the *expensis pagine ludi Corporis Christi*, as we have already noted. In 1378 fines incurred by the Bakers at York were divided between the city and *la pagine des ditz Pestour de corpore christi*.[50] At Coventry there is a reference to a pageant house for *le pagent pannarum* [drapers] *Coventre* as early as 1392. A number of unspecified references to pageants follow. But in the *Leet Book* in 1441 there is a specific order regulating actors which states that plays were a regular part of the feast of Corpus Christi.[51] Whatever form they took, the pageants listed at Hereford in 1501 were 'for the procession of Corpus Christi'. Traditionally it used to be held that the Latin plays which were part of the liturgical year were collected after the institution of the feast of Corpus Christi in 1311, translated into the vernacular, and presented as an integral part of the day's festivities. However, there was no reason to detach the Latin plays from their place in the liturgy, where they performed an integral part of the particular celebration with which they were connected. Because this theory has been so widespread, and accords in fact so ill with the probable sequence of events, I feel it worthwhile at this point to summarize V. A. Kolve's reconstruction of the most probable development of the feast of Corpus Christi as an occasion for medieval English drama. For his reconstruction has an important influence on how we view the records of early mobile pageant stages, particularly at York, the city long held to exemplify the method of producing the Corpus Christi mystery cycles in medieval England.

First, as to the relation of the Latin drama to the liturgy. Because earlier historians of the drama had the habit of lumping together references to individual dramatic performances at various locations, it was made to appear that all the ingredients for a complete cycle could be found in the liturgical celebrations of any large religious centre. Kolve, however, points out that 'Not only did most churches having Latin drama have only one or two short plays, but most often they had the *same* plays (that is, plays devoted to the same subjects); the repertoire of plays available in any given city was generally small'.[52] At York Minster, for example, only the plays of the Shepherds and of the Three Kings—the *Pastores* and the *Stella*—were ever presented.

At Lincoln, as indicated earlier there was a wide range of vernacular drama. In the cathedral, however, fairly complete records indicate that a limited number of plays were presented during the liturgical year, virtually without change for over two hundred years. The first play of which we have any record is a play of the Three Kings on the feast of Epiphany, in 1317. To this was added after 1321 a play *de sancto Thoma didimo*, probably a *Peregrini* play on Christ's appearances to his disciples. Subsequently, toward the end of the fourteenth century, these plays were displaced (references to them drop out of the records) by a dramatization of the Annunciation, and in the fifteenth century by a rather elaborate play on the Assumption of the Virgin. These two plays, dramatizing the beginning and the end of the adult life of the Virgin, to whom the cathedral was dedicated, continued to be presented in what must have been the same form until the middle of the sixteenth century. Clearly the Latin liturgical drama, though spread widely over England and the continent, was nevertheless scanty in any given community. 'This situation never radically altered simply because the house of God has its continuing concern with sacramental worship, not with dramatic mimesis.'[53] The Latin plays, at rest in the cycle of the church year, represented a dramatic form which entirely fulfilled its function, and had no inherent internal reason for further development.

The institution of the feast of Corpus Christi throughout Europe in 1311 provided an occasion for a new dramatic impulse, however. When Pope Urban IV first proposed such a feast in 1264, his reasons for doing so had an important consequence in the subsequent forms of celebration which developed for this feast. The feast is intended to focus all its attention on the Holy Sacrament of the Mass. To be sure the service of Maundy Thursday celebrates the institution of the Holy Sacrament at the Last Supper. 'But Urban instituted a feast date that was not an anniversary so that this maximum gift could be celebrated separately (Maundy Thursday is overcrowded with significant events) and, more important, so that this gift from God of Himself might be a source of rejoicing.'[54] Rejoicing is hardly the proper mood for the evening of the betrayal in the garden, but it is nevertheless the proper mood for celebrating the Holy Sacrament once Easter is past. Once Pentecost is over, the sequence of services which early developed around the final appearances of Christ to his disciples ends, and the doldrums of the church year sets in until Advent. Into this period, in the period between 23 May and 24 June (depending on the date of the celebration of Easter) the feast of Corpus Christi was inserted. It is not there, be it noted, because it is a period of good weather in Europe, and thus suitable for outdoor dramatic performances. It is there because the church calendar was not full at that time of the year. Only a procession leading up to celebration of the Mass is specified as part of the feast. The plays developed later.[55]

In preparing plays for such an occasion, one could have dramatized the power of the Holy Sacrament through plays presenting miracles of the Host. Many of these occur in the *exempla* collections which were drawn on for sermons for Corpus Christi day. Such a play, the Croxton *Play of the Sacrament*, even survives in England. However, this play, written apparently for a travelling troupe, is not associated with the feast of Corpus Christi. Rather it appears to be an anti-Lollard vindication of the doctrine of the Real Presence. Instead of such dramatized miracles to celebrate the feast, English cities chose instead plays representing the history of the world, from Creation to Doomsday, in which a crucial event is the institution of the Holy Sacrament.

The Eucharist serves to recall both the Last Supper and the flesh and blood of Christ offered on the cross—events about which it is possible to rejoice only when they are related to man's fall, Christ's Resurrection, and the Last Judgment. Except for this sacrifice and gift, even the good would have been damned, guilty of Adam's sin. To play the whole story, then, is in the deepest sense to *celebrate* the Corpus Christi sacrament, to explain its necessity and power, and to show how that power will be made manifest at the end of the world.[56]

The events and characters chosen for representation which recur consistently wherever sequences of pageants are named for a Corpus Christi celebration are as follows: The Fall of Lucifer, The Creation and Fall of Man, Cain and Abel, Noah and the Flood, Abraham and Isaac, The Nativity (Annunciation to Jesus and the Doctors), The Raising of Lazarus (the only Ministry play staged by all cycles), The Passion (Conspiracy to Harrowing of Hell), The Resurrection (Setting of the Watch to the Ascension), and Doomsday. To these may be added a group of plays which occur in all but one of the surviving lists: Moses (Exodus, or Laws, or both), The Prophets, The Baptism, The Temptation, The Assumption and Coronation of the Virgin.[57] The Old Testament plays selected are there because they prefigure the events in the New Testament which surround the institution of the Eucharist. Later additions to the basic cycle form were of course made. For example, the Lincoln Cathedral play of the Assumption of the Virgin was joined to the Corpus Christi cycle put on by the city. But this is the basic form.

How it came about that English celebrations of the feast of Corpus Christi most often chose to represent the scenes in this sequence of events we do not know. Somehow that choice was made. But I cannot insist sufficiently strongly that the choice was made within the context of a procession which wound through the village, town, or city, in which the leading citizens took assigned positions in the procession wearing full regalia, often organized by craft guilds, and in which there was an elaborately decorated feretory containing the Host. This procession's goal was the church or cathedral, where the Holy Sacrament was celebrated as the culmination of the procession. Without the final celebration, the feast was pointless. It should be added that so long as the feast of Corpus Christi continued to exert any influence on the cycles represented, the terms 'religious' as opposed to 'secular' are meaningless. When the town of Louth instituted a Corpus Christi cycle in the early sixteenth century, as part of their celebration of the feast of Corpus Christi, they did so as an act of devotion. When the plays were finally put down in Elizabeth's reign, it was because they represented too well the religious life of England's pre-Reformation past.

Certainly until the form of the Corpus Christi cycles had become well-established, the units of the basic sequence were all a necessary part of any presentation of the cycle. But the manner of representation need not initially always have been fully dramatic. As early as 1298 the Fishmongers had carried 'amongest other Pageants and shews foure Sturgeons guilt, carried on foure horses: then foure Salmons of silver on foure horses' followed by forty-six knights on horses 'made like Luces of the sea', with one dressed as St Magnus because the procession celebrating Edward I's victory was on St Magnus' day.[58] In an age when so much of the material of the Corpus Christi cycle was already familiar in stone and glass, as well as in the sermon literature of the period, visual representation of the separate units of the cycle would certainly elicit an understanding response in any onlookers. Indeed the series of events in York in the late fourteenth century suggests much more a gradual movement from *tableaux vivants* taking part in the Corpus Christi procession, to pageant wagons as sets for plays not dissimilar from the ones we now possess, than it suggests a cycle with fully developed plays in existence before 1376. Inasmuch as the pattern at York has been applied so generally to the rest of England, it is perhaps worth pointing out a few reasons why the development I have suggested may in fact have taken place.

To begin with there is the matter of the statutes regulating the stations at which the pageants were presented. We will remember from the royal entry in Coventry that the audience there was in two parts, a secondary part stationary, grouped at the various stages, watching as much the show presented by the passing sovereign as the show on the stages. The primary audience, however, moved from station to station; and at each station a single performance was given. A religious procession is itself like the royal entry at Coventry; scenes represented within that procession must be for a stationary audience. Apparently at York the audience had developed stations, probably those at which the Host in the Corpus Christi procession was exhibited in its elaborate feretory, at which the pageants in procession periodically halted.[59] But in 1394 there was an order passed requiring the pageants to play at the assigned places and not elsewhere, suggesting that all was not working as it should be. In 1399 there was still trouble over the stations; in that year the commons petitioned the town council 'that, as they are at great cost about *le juer et les pagentz de la iour de corpore cristi*, which were not performed as they ought to be on account of there being too many places, the number of these should be limited to twelve'.[60] Twelve places were in use in 1417, probably the same stations as were established in response to the complaint of the commons in 1399. Apparently thereafter one could arrange to have a station at one's home or place of business if one paid enough.[61] This implies that provision was being made for the audience at such stations, and that admission of some sort was being charged to make a profit from the lease. The number of stations had grown to sixteen by 1542, and provided a considerable sum to the city treasury.[62]

It has always been assumed that, from the time of the earliest references to these pageants and stations at York, the plays as we have them were all produced annually, with the procession assembling at four-thirty in the morning, and with each play being enacted on each pageant wagon at each station, finishing at sunset, if all went well. A recently completed statistical study of the actual time needed to perform the plays as we have them indicates that the plays as they survive could not possibly have been put on in their entirety at the twelve stations, much less the sixteen, in one day.[63] There simply was not enough time to do it; for example, the thirteenth play could not begin until the twelfth had finished playing at the first station before the priory of Holy Trinity in Mickelgate. Nor could any play advance till the longest then playing finished. As the plays in the Ashburnham manuscript vary considerably in length, much time would be spent waiting for the longer plays to end, at each station in succession. The problems posed in this study exist in their most acute form at York, as it happens. Chester took three days for its cycle, and had fewer stations; Coventry seems to have had no more than three stations. Both cycles are shorter, and have fewer plays. We do not know what happened in Wakefield, and the plays themselves seem to have been written for a different situation than that prevailing in York.[64] The N-Town cycle does not conform to the York pattern at all. Nevertheless some explanation of what happened at York is needed. For the time being I would propose the following solution to the problem.

Let us take the procession first. In 1426 a monk named Melton persuaded the townspeople to separate the procession from the plays which had grown up within it in order to preserve the sanctity of the procession. Thereafter the plays were put on on the day before the procession, not, as Craig states,[65] on the day of the festival. Thus it is only after 1426 that there would even have been a full day available as playing time. Prior to that date the focus of the festivities on Corpus Christi day was the celebration of the Mass. This means that prior to 1426 there would have been great pressure for a total playing time of not more than six hours, that is, if there was to be time for Mass before noon.

Analogous to the medieval procession in York is a modern parade such as the Memorial Day parades common in the United States or the Lord Mayor's show in London. Occasionally along the route of such parades a group or organization will erect a scaffold, or set of 'bleachers', much as the citizens of York erected their twelve or more stations. People are free to stand in front of these scaffolds along the street, but anyone who has ever attended a parade knows the advantage of even six inches of elevation. What happens in the modern instance is as follows. Everyone watching *sees* every band and/or float that passes. Some bands they *hear*, briefly, as they march past. Occasionally the parade halts. If the band is playing at that moment, the spectators *hear and see* more of the music. Suppose that the Corpus Christi procession began with every pageant wagon in order as we have them in the surviving manuscript of the plays, every wagon stage carrying its performers, at five in the morning. Suppose that the procession advanced till all the stations were occupied by a play and that the procession then halted, at which time *every* pageant acted out its bit in full, having simply mimed it up until that point. When all had finished, all would move on. It is worth noting in this connection that a copy of an order

of council of 1394, made by the town clerk, Burton, in 1415, includes
the stipulation, after the notice that players are to be on their pageants
between four and five in the morning, that 'all other pageants fast
followyng ilk one after other as ther course is, without tarieng'.[66]
Some sort of close order was certainly preserved as much as
possible.

How many times would each play have been put on? A later order
of 3 April 1476, perhaps provides the answer. This order reads, in part,

And that no plaier that shall plaie in the saide Corpus X^{ti} plaie be conducte
and reteyned to plaie but twise on the day of the saide playe; and that he or
thay so plaing plaie not ouere twise the saide day, vpon payne of xls. to forfet
vnto the chaumbre as often tymes as he or thay shall be founden defautie in
the same.[67]

This has traditionally been taken to prohibit doubling, but we need not
take it so. What it says is that no player is to act more than twice.
Does this not suggest that no play was put on in full at more than two
stations, for the obvious reason that there was not time for more?
Would not the actors with the more popular plays be likely to want to
put on their play as often as possible, to the detriment of the pageant
wagons following?

The result of such a procedure would be that everyone would be able
to enjoy the colour and excitement of the elaborate pageant wagons,
they would see all the scenes in the cycle, and perceive as much of the
unity of the conception as they would from stained-glass windows,
or wall paintings, except that these representations would more often
than not be *tableaux vivants*. If they were willing to pay their penny,
they would be given seats to see some of the tableaux come more fully
to life. Hence the constant concern for pageants playing only at the
assigned stations. There would, after all, be real temptation if one were
part of a short, rather pedestrian play behind a longer, more exciting
one, to go into one's routine while waiting in the street for a turn to
move on, either before or after coming to a station. And those who saw
that performance would not have paid for the privilege.

During the time when such conditions of production prevailed, if
this in fact is anything like the actual state of affairs, all plays would be
short, and of about the same length. However, once the town, following Friar William's suggestion in 1426, had separated the plays from
the procession, then the cycle would be much freer to expand, with the
whole day to work in. The expanded plays, particularly the work of the

York Realist, would then fall after 1426, which they seem to do on
other grounds, as we have already noted.[68]

The reason we have got into the habit of thinking of each cycle as
being put on in its entirety nearly every year, is that we know that the
pageant wagons were used every year. But if they were got out and
manned for the procession, but not all used for acting upon, we would
not know it from the surviving records. The York text, a register of all
plays available for Corpus Christi day, need not bear any relation to
the plays produced in any one year. Inasmuch as the playbooks we do
have seem to be registers rather than collections of working copies,
we would expect them to contain all the plays that the particular town
considered worth producing—hence the two Shepherds' plays at
Wakefield. Certainly none of the surviving texts represent the actual
state of affairs in, say, York, in 1397 during the visit of Richard II.
The most we can say is that the plays we have were all produced at
some time before they became part of the registers.

Plays presented at a series of stations are most often called *processional*
by modern scholars, though the users of this term generally deny that
the plays have anything to do with the Corpus Christi procession itself.
Alternatively we can use the term *station-to-station* or *stop-to-stop* to
describe such plays. Once a pageant wagon is stopped, it becomes
effectively the same as a permanent, fixed stage. One can really only
call a moving *tableau vivant* a processional stage if by the term is meant
'a stage processing'. I myself prefer *station-to-station*, and shall use it
hereafter. It is the attempt to perform the cycles of Corpus Christi
plays at a sequence of separate locations rather than at a single spot
that distinguishes the two major types of medieval drama in England.
Wagons which had taken part in a Corpus Christi procession as floats,
and which were then moved into a large acting area to serve as sup-
plementary stages in conjunction with fixed scaffolds, all of them
surrounding or backing a *platea* or 'place', are functioning as place-
and-scaffold stages.[69]

This can best be illustrated by the N-Town cycle play of Noah, a
play originally written for station-to-station production. From the
point of view of character development this is one of the least interesting of the Noah plays. Noah's wife is as devout as he is, as are all his
children. After Noah has made a statement of faith, God (speaking
from some unspecified spot, in this cycle a permanent Heaven scaffold)
sends an angel to notify Noah of his task. As soon as the message is
received, the following stage direction appears: 'Here Noah leaves

with his family for the ship, he having left the place of the interlude,
let Lamech enter below immediately led by a boy and say—.'[70] There
follows the curious and unique episode of Lamech, a blind hunter,
shooting once more in his old age to prove his skill with the bow and
arrow, at a mark indicated by a boy.[71] He kills Cain, who had been
hiding in a bush on stage.[72] Realizing that he has incurred God's
curse on the slayer of Cain, he beats the boy to death with his bow
and exits to this stage direction: 'Here let Lamech retire and immediately let Noah enter with the ship, all singing.'[73] The Lamech episode
is there to cover the time needed for Noah and his family to exit and
climb into the pageant ship waiting off-stage.[74] Those privileged to see
the performance of this play in the production at Grantham in 1966
know that the subsequent entrance of the pageant ship is marvellously
effective, far more so than any attempt to construct a ship on stage, as
in the Chester cycle. A live audience *knows* why the Lamech episode
is there, and accepts it for what it is, a bit of theatrical business of the
sort performed before the curtain during a scene change in a revue.
When the ship's business is over, it leaves, with its occupants once more
singing.

Pageant wagons of the ark are among the most elaborate made.
Rents for their storage are always more than for other wagons.
Certainly they took part in the procession at the feast of Corpus Christi.
But it would be ridiculous to call the N-Town ark a 'processional
stage' simply because it processes into the *locum interludij*. This is an
imaginative adjustment of a kind of stage inherited from the fourteenth-
century processions to a later form of staging, and characterizes the
plays in the N-Town cycle. Similar adjustments appear to have taken
place in the Wakefield cycle, but on this topic there is still considerable
dispute. What is safest to say is that at York, Coventry, and Chester
we know that a serious attempt was made to preserve station-to-
station staging of the Corpus Christi plays. Elsewhere place-and-
scaffold staging appears to have been the rule.

Certainly we know that the Cornish plays were produced in a
place-and-scaffold setting. Diagrams similar to that in the *Castle of
Perseverance* appear both in the *Ordinalia* and the life of St Meriasek.
London, where plays about saints' lives and Passion plays were being
produced in the late twelfth century, had a cycle play presented by the
clerks of London in the late fourteenth century. We really know almost
nothing about the content of the cycle, other than the fact that it did
comprise scenes from the Old and New Testament in 1391, and that as

presented in 1409 it extended from the Creation to the Last Judgment. In 1384, 1391, and 1409 the play lasted four days, but seven in 1411. All the notices of these productions mention them as taking place at a single location, Skinners' Well. So large a production, regularly utilizing the same location, and that a permanent architectural feature, must certainly have been of the place-and-scaffold type, particularly where the court was so much influenced by French artistic styles.

Richard Southern has amply demonstrated not only how effectively the place-and-scaffold theatre is employed in the *Castle of Perseverance*, but also, in his preliminary discussion, how much the terminology of place-and-scaffold staging permeates the stage directions of that play. The diagram siting the scaffolds used in the play around a circular playing area is one of the most familiar medieval theatrical diagrams. Kenneth Cameron and I have indicated elsewhere how completely the N-Town cycle has been adapted to just such a theatre, though perhaps one arranged in a semi-circle or with a line of scaffolds as at Valenciennes rather than in a circle.[75] Both of these long plays come from the same general area of England, as already noted. Norwich is traditionally supposed to have had a cycle, albeit an unusually short one. However, the 1527 entry in the Proceedings of the Norwich Assembly, when read carefully, established in fact that prior to 1527 the St Luke's Guild, a city-wide religious guild similar to the St Anne's Guild at Lincoln which also supervised plays, had been responsible for putting on not a cycle at all but something with which we are by now quite familiar. Prior to 1527 this guild had been responsible for

diuers disgisinges and pageauntes as well of the liff and marterdams of diuers and many hooly sayntes as also many other lyght and feyned figures, pictures of other persones and bestes, the sight of which disgisinges and pageauntes, as well yerly on the said Monday in Pentecost Weke in tyme of procession than goyng aboute a grete circuitt of the said Citie, as yerly the Tuysday in the same weke seruyng of the lord named the Lord of Mysrule at Tomlond within the same Citie.[76]

This surely is a procession of pageants but not of plays; Norwich had a Corpus Christi procession at least from 1489, when an order for the procession is recorded, but the list of pageants for the Norwich cycle appears to date from as late as 1533, when the order of the procession was revised.[77] The records Davis prints appear to indicate that the pageant wagons were got out for the procession on Corpus Christi day, but that such a play as the surviving Norwich Grocers' play was

most probably produced on Monday in Whit week, as a replacement
for the older 'disgisinges and pageauntes'. Such a production does not
suggest station-to-station staging.

All the remaining plays of some size discussed in Chapter 1 are of
the place-and-scaffold type. The Digby play of *Mary Magdalene* seems
particularly to be drawing on all possible theatrical uses of the place-
and-scaffold stage, including several appearances of a ship much like
the ark in the N-Town cycle. Local records from Essex indicate that
place-and-scaffold staging was in use in the cycle play at Chelmsford,
where scaffolding for a temple and a Hell-Mouth was erected as part
of the preparations in the church.[78] Giles Dawson has recently edited
a set of fascinating accounts having to do with a place-and-scaffold
Corpus Christi play at New Romney—all late, to be sure, but still
of great interest.[79] The situation in England thus appears to correspond surprisingly closely to that recently surveyed in Spain by N. D.
Shergold. In his *History of the Spanish Stage*, Shergold has noted that
in Mallorca and Catalonia one finds considerable evidence of simultaneous staging of the place-and-scaffold variety for the religious
drama.[80] These are the areas most influenced by Provençal culture.
On the other hand, in Barcelona and Valencia where French influence
was much less pronounced there is a tradition of pageantry associated
with the Corpus Christi procession in which the plays make a very late
appearance. *Tableaux vivants* there are the rule until the early sixteenth
century.

Barcelona is of particular interest, for the celebration of Corpus
Christi Day there has many interesting parallels with English practices.
In 1424 a list of the procession was prepared, containing 108 different
scenes, presented by almost every organized body, religious or secular,
in the city. This list simply gives the order of the procession, and the
scenes. An edict from 1448, however, seeks to prescribe the places
where the organizers of the festivity were to hold 'performances and
sports' (*representacions e jochs*).[81] On the basis of a document dated
20 April 1453, Shergold has been able to deduce the kind of performances regulated five years earlier. In 1453 Johan Calom, a prebendary
of the city, agreed to provide new pageants, called *entramesos* of the
Creation, the Nativity, and the Annunciation.

The Creation of the World was to consist of a heaven of clouds supported on
four pillars [i.e. a wagon with a roof] with angels and God the Father, the latter
with an orb in his right hand. Between Heaven and the platform of the float
was to hang a great round globe, half of which was to be painted as water, and

the other half to be part stars, and part land, with a city on it. The pageant of
the Nativity was also to have pillars, on which were to be four angels holding
up a round, or domed, heaven with stars and clouds, in the middle of which was
God the Father, as in the other. Rays of fire or light were to descend from God
to the infant Jesus, who was to be seen naked in the manger, with the ox and
the ass near by, and Joseph and Mary kneeling on each side. Rays of light
passed from them to the child. Above, the angels sang *Gloria in excelsis*. It
was at this point that the actual 'performance' took place, for the Magi were
to ride up on horseback, dismount, and go up the steps of the float to adore the
child. There is no indication, however, that there was any dialogue, and the
scene on the float resembles a religious picture rather than the scenery for
a play.[82]

The appeal here is entirely visual, with action of a theatrical nature
enhancing the presentation of traditional religious scenes. Calom
agreed to provide a theatrical effect for the performance of the Annunciation as well. There he was to arrange for a dove to descend from
the Father's mouth to Mary, and return, 'moving its wings'. In addition there were to be rays of light, or fire (which did no damage).
The same theatrical effect without the dove was specified in the N-
Town cycle, as it happens.

The existence of two dramatic traditions in Spain, one place-and-
scaffold, deriving much of its conventions from the medieval drama
of France, and one station-to-station, developing from theatrical shows
presented on pageant wagons drawn in the Corpus Christi procession,
thus exactly parallels the situation we have been positing in England.
It is in the areas most remote from the Continent, such as York and
Chester, that the station-to-station method of staging persists in its
clearest form until the end of the Corpus Christi plays. At York the
other forms of drama, the Paternoster play and the Creed play, appear
to have conformed to the station-to-station form of staging as well.
But in the East Midlands and the South the staging developed for the
Jeu d'Adam appears to have been preferred. The majority of the surviving plays from these areas are of this type, whether Corpus Christi
cycles, moralities, or dealing with saints' lives. At Coventry only the
very late *Destruction of Jerusalem*, produced after 1584, appears to have
been of the place-and-scaffold type. All references to scaffolds in the
Coventry records are after that date. On the other hand, the plays in
the Wakefield cycle seem so consistently to indicate the use of the
wagons in a single playing area that we must use the conventions of the
place-and-scaffold theatre to discuss these plays. It does no good to talk

of one method of staging as dominant in late medieval English drama. Rather we must remember the possibilities in the two major stage traditions, note the probable location of the plays in which we are most interested, and read them with the appropriate stage in mind. To such readings it is now time to turn.

3

DRAMATIC POSSIBILITIES

At their best the plays written for the medieval English stages are as good as any modern plays. Pageant wagon plays compare well with modern one-act dramas. For full appreciation of their continuing power it is probably best to continue to stage them in as focussed an area as their original environment.[1]

An excellent example of what a pageant wagon play can achieve is provided in the play of the York Thatchers, entitled in L. T. Smith's edition *The Journey to Bethlehem; the birth of Jesus*.[2] Such a title is immediately misleading. The play does not begin with Luke's narrative recounting the reasons why Joseph, of the lineage of the house of David, had to return to his family's city to be taxed. Station-to-station plays restrict the amount of journeying involved. What there is is represented by the briefest stage crossing. For example, in the Chandler's play of *The Angels and the Shepherds*, which follows immediately in the York cycle, once the angelic message has been given, the text gives the stage direction 'then they sing' (*tunc cantant*) (l. 85) following the suggestion of the third shepherd that they seek their Saviour with song. The speech immediately following the stage direction begins 'Breder, bees all blythe and glad, / Here is the burght there we chulde be' (l. 86–7). The amount of time taken up by singing of course could vary depending on the distance from the fields to the manger, but certainly no hard and fast length is implied by covering dialogue, as we regularly get in place-and-scaffold plays.

So the York Nativity play begins in Bethlehem, as they are seeking shelter. Joseph's first speech locates the play, if the sight of a stylized manger containing images of the traditional ox and ass as part of the wagon's decor, had not already done so. 'Lorde, graunte vs gode

herberow this night / within this wone' (ll. 6–7) prays Joseph. The two
were last seen, on the preceding stage, resolving *Joseph's Trouble About
Mary* in a scene of forgiveness sought and given. There the location had
clearly been Joseph's house in Nazareth. The journey to Bethlehem
takes place off-stage, then, so to speak. One can visualize the wagon
rolling into position with the figures on it static. As soon as it stops,
and the audience's attention settles down, the figures come alive, and
identify their quandary. It is worthwhile noting that no extraneous
people are on this stage; no inn-keepers, for example. Nor do any of
the popular midwives of the Chester or the N-Town cycle later appear.
The focus here is entirely on the Holy Family.

The playwright focusses his play even more intensely, however, once
the opening dialogue is complete. Mary and Joseph choose the stable
promptly, within thirty-eight lines. Joseph must simply hand Mary
into the stable. This need be no more than an arch, with the animals
facing the manger at its centre. So I constructed it in a performance of
this play I directed, staged in the choir of a medium-sized modern neo-
Gothic church on the Sunday after Christmas. This setting is quite
sufficient for the play's purposes. At this point Joseph retires, leaving
Mary alone in the stable. In the Chester and the N-Town plays, Joseph
departs to get the midwives, with whom he returns. Here the reason he
gives for departing is that he must obtain heat and light. The actual
reason for the exit, however, is given by Joseph in the N-Town cycle—
'It is not conuenyent a man to be / ther women gon in travalynge'
(ll. 133–4). Finally, it really is very hard to imagine what sort of business one would give Joseph during the actual birth, which probably
accounts as much as anything else for his absence.

In any case, Mary is alone, and onstage, for the birth of Christ. No
stage directions tell us how this was done. Undoubtedly a doll figure
was used. But how? At York, in the '50s, E. Martin Browne had Mary
wear a loose-fitting gown or cape. Under the gown was placed the
doll. Around the outside of the gown was tied a sash, with the knot in
front. Mary needed only to bend low, facing the audience, loosen the
sash, and remove the doll from under her skirt. This, or something
very like it, seems to me the best solution to the problem. In directing
the play, it is the procedure I followed. A paediatrician testified later
to the shock he had felt as, watching the play, he fully realized for the
first time that Christ was born like any other human child. Nothing

---

wone dwelling

in any picture, any sermon, had so brought that fact home to him. Under these circumstances, concealing the baby in the straw of the manger, as was done at the otherwise fine staging of the N-Town Nativity at Grantham, is not as effective. Straw sticks to the doll, and destroys the verisimilitude. For if the play is as focussed as it is at York, the audience's whole attention is directed to the fact of the Nativity. The theatrical illusion of a real birth must be as nearly right as can be, without resorting to obstetrical details which would deprive Mary of her dignity.

Once the birth has occurred, Mary's total love for her child in a birth traditionally without pain is expressed with simplicity and dignity. But the tenderness of such a moment is hard to sustain. Held for too long, it becomes saccharine. At just the right moment Joseph returns, underlining with his grumbling the fact that it is December, and dreadful weather. On the wagon stage, he has simply retired, crouched, and frozen in place—and thus disappeared. It is no agreed-upon convention, shared by audience and actors alike, that accomplishes this, but a fact of such stages that if an actor freezes well away from the action, he has in fact disappeared as effectively as if he had walked through a door. Joseph can walk off-stage (as a modern director will probably have him do), but he need not have done so in fifteenth-century York. His entrance builds beautifully toward his recognition of the birth of Christ, from the grumble at the cold, through the cheerful, homely greeting 'A, here be god, for nowe come I' (l. 83) to the first sight—'O Marie! what swete thyng is that on thy kne?' (l. 87)—to delight, but puzzlement at the strange light he perceives in the stable (here probably not recreated, though at Barcelona some theatrical effect had certainly been sought), to full recognition and worship. The play then moves to involve the beasts. Mary, having wrapped the child in 'such clothes as we haue here' (l. 121—her own shawl is most effective), lays the child between the ox and ass, where Mary and Joseph remark on the fact that the beasts are keeping the child warm with their breath. Joseph also notes that in doing so, they are fulfilling the prophecy of Habbakkuk that 'oure sauyoure shall be sene / betwene bestis lye' (l. 140). The play concludes with Joseph and Mary, probably framing the manger, praying to Christ for his blessing.

The economy of this play is perfect. No extraneous line is included, no detail distracts. The tone of the language is modulated to the action, and suits it exactly. In 154 lines the Nativity takes place in one of the finest realizations in medieval English drama.

For contrast, the Chester Wrights' play of the Salutation and
Nativity is singularly crowded and diffuse in its effect.[3] Not only does
it include the Salutation, which involves a long explication of the
Magnificat (possibly defensible as effective instruction of the laity,
but hardly tightly-constructed drama), but also *Joseph's Trouble with
Mary* in fifty-five lines, followed by 223 lines devoted to the edict of
Caesar, here called Octavian, that all the world should be taxed, as
well as Sibyl's prophecy. The Nativity itself is more concerned with
the miracle in which the midwife Salome, refusing to believe that a
maid could bear a child, touches Mary's vagina to determine whether
she is still a virgin, and suffers a withered hand for her disbelief. The
hand is cured when she seeks forgiveness from Christ. Finally the play
returns to Octavian and Sibyl, who see the star, as well as a vision of
the Virgin and Child, and worship appropriately. This is all interspersed with commentary by an Expositor, the whole occupying a total
of 736 lines.

Salter proposed that the Chester cycle was originally a single long
play, produced at one location, and interpreted as it went by the Expositor.[4] If the dispute in 1422 between the Carpenters and other guilds as to
who was to produce which play in fact concerns the play of the
Wrights, one can see here in the Wrights' Nativity play what may have
been an early form of pageant wagon play, though not yet one realizing effectively the potentialities of station-to-station production. In
fact, the play appears much more like a rather poor place-and-scaffold
play. Mary is located at some unspecified place at the beginning of the
play; in that location she is visited both by the angel, for the Annunciation, and by Elizabeth, for the Visitation. Then, according to a stage
direction, they go to Joseph (*tunc ibunt ad Ioseph*) (s.d. l. 120). If this is
all on a single stage, a short movement to the stationary figure of Joseph
would be sufficient. Joseph immediately launches into his accusation
that Mary has betrayed him, leaves her, sleeps, and receives his vision.
Where he is is not clear, but it is in the general area to which the
Emperor Octavian then goes. His entrance is typical of regal figures—
preceded by a messenger—who clears a way in the crowd. Inasmuch as
Octavian then conducts a long dialogue with his court and Sibyl, it
seems unlikely that he is at street level throughout this portion of the
play. In any case, the Emperor's messenger (called in the text *Preco*,
'crier') goes from the court to Joseph to announce the tax. Joseph in
turn first addresses the audience, and then, having turned to speak to
Mary, he ties the ox to the neck of the ass (he will sell the ox to raise

the tax), places Mary on the ass, and then goes to the stable. During the passage to the stable Mary remarks on the crowd, undoubtedly the spectators present at the play. Having arrived at the stable, Joseph takes Mary in his arms and then puts her between the two beasts, before leaving for the midwives. In this play the Nativity takes place during Joseph's absence, but here the focus is all on a dialogue between Joseph and the midwives. Upon Joseph's return, Mary shows him the child, and the events of the miracle then unfold. When Salome has been cured, the Expositor then fills in a number of patristic glosses on the preceding events, and narrates the story of the fall of the image in Rome at the time of the Nativity. Octavian and Sibyl then converse, and appear to see not only the star, which had appeared after the birth, but also the Virgin and Child. Octavian vows to bear incense to the child. The Expositor concludes with the tale that a church dedicated to Mary, called the *Ara Caeli*, was founded in Rome on the spot where Octavian had his vision.

Here is no focus: here are instead all the legends surrounding Christ's birth, lumped together with no sense of discrimination. Except for the curious use of the animals, all could be presented on a single pageant wagon stage, for no part of the play contains any action of any scope. It is rather as if each player, or group of players, were conceived of as not much more than one step beyond pictures. Here is the dramaturgy of the *tableau vivant*, extended somewhat by the arrival through the crowd of an Emperor with his court, plus the use of animals. But the animals appear to require two acting areas. Perhaps the bulk of the play took place on a scaffold, with the Nativity itself on a separate stage, perhaps the wagon of the Wrights. Otherwise we must posit all the action but the Nativity as taking place on audience level. This is, of course, certainly possible but highly unlikely.

Whether the play employed one or two raised acting areas is not really the point here. Rather I have included the discussion of the Chester Wrights' play as a step toward establishing standards by which we may judge the effectiveness of the cycle plays written for pageant wagon stages. Where the York Nativity play is concentrated, economic, and characterized by dialogue consistently appropriate to the action presented, the playwright constructing the Chester Wrights' play has no sense of form. There is no stage in the author's mind for which he is writing. Rather, he is intent on getting as many of the legends of the Nativity enacted as he can fit in, no matter how. And by 'enacted' is really meant 'said'. Different people 'say' the different

legends, but no one really acts out any of them. Thus we cannot even
reconstruct the staging of this play with any certainty, for the playwright had no very clear understanding of what constituted drama.
It is not really important whether this play is early or late, though I am
inclined to think that it is early. What is important is that to judge the
effectiveness of these early plays we use the same criteria that we would
apply to a play by Ibsen or Albee. Does the playwright have a feel for
his theatre; has he realized his material in a form which is appropriate
for that theatre? The narrow bounds of the pageant wagon stage
become a glass through which we can focus on the fact of the York
Nativity. Any space which focusses the attention of the audience in
the same way is an appropriate setting for this play. It should not sur-
prise anyone, therefore, to learn that one criterion for judging the
effectiveness of medieval English drama is the degree to which it
realizes the potentialities of the stage for which that particular play was
written.

Defining the qualities which distinguish superior plays of the place-
and-scaffold type is never a simple task, inasmuch as such plays in-
variably run to some length. Utilizing separate raised acting areas
connected by a central open area on audience level, they characteristically depend for much of their effect on processions from stage to stage.
Thus, in the *Castle of Perseverance*, certainly one of the earliest surviving
plays in this form, we find that the action begins almost immediately
with such movement. The debate between *Humanum Genus* and his
Good and Bad Angels leads directly to the movement from the
World's stage of Lust, Liking (i.e., Desire), and Folly to assist the Bad
Angel in tempting Mankind. Mankind's 'fall' is in fact accomplished
by his physical movement across the place to World's scaffold, and his
decision to join the forces of evil located there.

In effect, when someone decides to do something in this theatre,
the decision is dramatized by movement to a new location. Thus, in
addition to the normal range of actions that can take place on or around
a raised acting area, from Noah's fight to get his wife up into his ark
in the Wakefield cycle, to the full-scale siege of the Castle of Perseverance, complete with mining operations and an attempted fire set
against the castle wall, we also have messengers running back and forth
between potentates, courts moving to join other courts, or figures
such as Christ being dragged back and forth between the courts of
Pilate and Herod. In this theatre something is always happening, for it
is a theatre of movement. The temptation, of course, is to introduce

movement for its own sake, journeys for the sake of the spectacle rather than for any other dramatic purpose. The ship which takes Mary Magdalene to Marseilles (in the saint's life by that name in the Digby manuscript) is also used to take the King of Marseilles to Jerusalem and back so that he may be baptized by Peter. His wife apparently dies *en route*, and is abandoned on a rock. On the return journey, the queen and child are found alive, retrieved from the rock, and return to Marseilles. After this the stage direction reads 'Here goth the shep out ofe the place'.[5] To be sure this is a miracle wrought by the Magdalene, but its presence in the play seems to be governed largely by the fact that there was available a movable ship which made a spectacular prop. Here is an example of the theatrical possibilities of the place-and-scaffold staging dictating the content, rather than the content using the theatrical possibilities to dramatize a particular point.

One of the most imaginative uses of place-and-scaffold staging in late medieval English drama occurs in the N-Town cycle.[6] The cycle itself is a composite, and contains plays written for station-to-station staging, left pretty much as they were handed down from the past, as well as a group of plays on the life of the Virgin which were for the most part written for the wagon stages, but apparently adapted to production in a single location as part of a place-and-scaffold production. At the centre of the cycle, however, are a group of plays dealing with the Passion which were clearly written with the place-and-scaffold stage in mind. Lack of space prevents me from analyzing the characteristics of the entire sequence, extending from the Council of the Jews prior to the entry into Jerusalem until after the Crucifixion. However, following the betrayal in the garden of Gethsemane, and some short concluding material, there follows a prologue spoken by 'an exposytour in doctorys wede' who also provided transitions in the Marian cycle. He indicates that the material from the Entry through the Betrayal was put on in the preceding year. We can therefore treat this as a self-contained whole, a play intended to be presented as a comprehensible single unit.[7] It is to this body of material that I now wish to turn.

First let us visualize the stations required for this play. A number of locations or scaffolds are directly indicated in the text.[8] To begin with, both Annas and Caiphas have their own scaffolds. The first full stage direction opens with the instruction 'Here shal annas shewyn hymself in his stage . . .' (p. 230, s.d. l. 40). The next stage direction provides that 'cayphas shewyth himself in his skafhald' (p. 232, s.d. l. 44). Both, then, require separate structures, probably of the type familiar from the illustration of the martyrdom of St Appollonia, a raised stage with a curtained enclosure on its rear half, having a ladder extending down to the ground on its front or side.[9] Because their scaffolds are some distance apart, I have placed them on opposite sides of the semi-circular arrangement. The next structure indicated is 'a lytil oratory' which should be in 'the myd place . . . with stolys and cusshonys clenly beseyn lyche as it were a cownsel hous' (p. 235, s.d. l. 124). This is the same location as that specified for the castle in the *Castle of Perseverance*, as well as Galilee and Emmaus in the *Seinte Resurreccion*.[10] Such a structure would almost certainly be at ground level. A fourth location is needed for the ass and her foal, for Christ sends his disciples to 'yon castel' (p. 237, l. 183) for the animals. This structure can be used for Jerusalem as well, and the four citizens who form the Palm Sunday crowd, as well as the children involved, could then issue from this structure. As a Castle of Emmaus is employed in the later Passion play, it seems probable that a castle is used here because one was available. The fifth structure specified is the house of Simon the Leper. This must be to the rear of the acting area, and raised, and of sufficient size to accommodate the Last Supper. Next there is the Mount of Olivet. Jesus goes 'to betany ward' (p. 262, s.d. l. 892) after the Last Supper. This is the general area in which Olivet is located. The mountain is used by Christ for prayer, and apparently includes several trees at its base, for the text specifies that 'a lytyl ther besyde' there is a place 'lyche to a park' (p. 262, s.d. l. 908). In view of what we have determined about the kinds of structures used in street pageants, and the ubiquity of mountains in medieval and Renaissance pageants, it seems probable that the angel who descends to give Christ the Eucharist during the Agony appears from the top of the mountain. The descent could be either on foot, or by mechanical means. There is almost certainly a temple in which Mary is located, and to which Magdalene goes at the conclusion of the play. A temple is required for Mary in the second Passion play, for a Latin stage direction there reads *Tunc transiet maria ad templum* . . (p. 305, s.d. l. 962). I have therefore included one in the diagram. Finally, in view of the periodic appearances of a demon, a Hell Mouth on far stage left is necessary.

These structures could be located around the periphery of a circle or in a semi-circle using the front of a cathedral or church as a sounding board to the rear. In view of the visual effect which is demanded in this play, of the action in the council house going on simultaneously and

The N-Town Passion Play I before Lincoln Cathedral (drawing
by Fred Warner)

contrasting with the Last Supper at Simon the Leper's, I am inclined to believe that a flattened semi-circular arrangement, with the council house at its geometrical centre, is what is required. Certainly the siting of the structures in a single two-dimensional plane as at Grantham is not appropriate. The accompanying diagram, therefore, is my own reconstruction of the staging specified in this play, and should be consulted as the analysis of the action proceeds.

The play opens with a prologue addressed to the audience by a demon figure. His actions and speech are exactly those of the Vice figures in the moralities, to which we will return later. Unlike the figure of Satan, who appears later, in the second Passion play, he is unnamed. Even though he is ostensibly the tempter of Christ in the Wilderness, his real function (aside from outlining the sequence of events to follow, leading up to the Betrayal) is to remind the audience that to fail to follow the way of Christ is to become a fellow of demons. For the real thrust of his speech is a disquisition on the ways of sin very much in the tradition of sermon literature on the seven deadly sins.[11] His description of the broad road to Hell is immediately contrasted with the narrow way leading to eternal life described by John the Baptist, who succeeds him on stage. St John's speech concludes with the summary statement, 'How ye shal aray the wey I haue made declaracion / Also the ryth patthis agens the comyng of oure lord' (p. 230, ll. 39–40). The action which follows has been given both its eternal and its contemporary dimension.

John has no sooner finished speaking than the curtain to Annas' scaffold is pulled open, revealing him in his splendid scarlet gown, cut like that of a bishop of the Old Law, covered with a blue tabard 'furryd with whyte', and wearing a mitre, also 'after the hoold lawe' (p. 230, s.d. l. 40). He is an imposing figure, flanked by his two doctors of the law, also elaborately costumed, and his messenger, costumed as a Saracen. Annas immediately identifies himself by name. Then, acting on the advice of his doctors of law, he sends his messenger to invite Caiphas, Rufin and Leon to a council to determine how to deal with the threat to the law constituted by Jesus. The following action is thus motivated, the succeeding characters and their functions are identified, and the movement between locations normal to this theatre is given the necessary plausibility. As the messenger, Arfexe, is climbing down to travel across to the scaffold of Caiphas, the second scaffold's curtains

---

aray prepare   *ryth patthis* straight ways

open, revealing a second set of elaborately costumed figures. Caiphas is to follow the costume for Annas, except that his tabard 'shall be red furryd with white' (p. 232, s.d. l. 44). He, too, is much concerned about the threat posed by Jesus but, just as he is about to consult with Annas, the messenger arrives, inviting him to the council. As the messenger speaks to Caiphas (from ground level?), Rufin and Leon walk into the place, wearing striped tabards and furred hoods. Thus as the messenger leaves the scaffold of Caiphas, he immediately finds the next group to whom he must speak available. Having given his message, he returns to Annas, who descends to the place, and joins the others who have all been moving toward the council house in the centre of the place. The play has begun, with bustle and colour, and an effective use of the normal conventions of this theatre.

The transition between the council and the next 'scene' is not spelled out as carefully in the manuscript as are most subsequent transitions because there has been an alteration at this point. An entrance provided for Peter and John the Baptist has been cancelled at the foot of folio 142 verso. The interpolated leaf which follows begins with a speech by Jesus. Thus we must turn to a later stage direction to understand what in fact happens at this point. Later when Jesus has entered the scaffold representing the house of Simon the Leper, the stage direction reads 'in the mene tyme the cownsel hous beforn-seyd shal sodeynly onclose schewyng the buschopys prestys and jewgys syttyng in here astat lyche as it were a convocacyone' (p. 245, s.d. l. 397). From this it is clear that the council of the Jews ends with curtains being drawn around the structure as Christ and his disciples enter the place. The entry of such a large group of actors would draw the audience's attention away from the council house. Once curtained off, the house becomes simply part of the scenery. The advantage of this device is apparent both at Christ's entrance into Jerusalem, and at his entrance into the house of Simon. Two large groups of people who are not supposed to see or speak to each other can be brought into action in quick succession without having to wait for a complete emptying and refilling of the large open playing area. The fast pace established at the outset is thus maintained, and excitement is generated by quick shifts between contrasting actions, both of which the audience knows will converge subsequently.

Christ enters directly into the place. At this point he indicates the 'castle' where the ass and the foal are tied. 'Burgesses' within the castle predictably question the taking of the animals, and then acquiesce.

Once Christ has mounted the ass, the text specifies that he should ride out of the place, leaving Peter and John the Baptist to preach a sermon to the 'people of Jerusalem'; i.e., the audience. Doctrinal instruction thus occurs naturally, within the flow of the action, rather than through the intrusion of an extraneous figure, as in the Chester *Sacrifice of Isaac*. John's reappearance in this role also underlines the short introductory sermon. Finally, the use of two speakers gives some added life to what must always be the least lively aspect of medieval drama.

Upon the conclusion of the sermon, four citizens appear, probably from the castle. They go bare-footed, in their shirts, with their gowns tied loosely about their waists so that they may lay them in Christ's path. Tree branches are also referred to in their dialogue, as well as flowers. The children who meet Jesus after he has passed the citizens carry flowers to strew before him. These are almost certainly choirboys, for they sing the *Gloria laus* as Jesus passes them. Two blind men appear and are healed, and finally Christ sheds tears for the future of Jerusalem. All of these actions make it possible to move the 'Entry into Jerusalem' completely around the place, circling in front of the council house, with each new group which meets the procession entering through the spaces between different scaffolds. Again the play makes maximum use of the potentialities of the open place, with sufficient variety to the procession for it to remain constantly exciting.

The procession halts near Simon's house, having circled around the council house on the audience's side of the theatre, with different groups successively involving the house in the action. When Christ finally enters Simon's house, the stage direction specifies that he and his disciples then 'ete the paschal lamb' (p. 245, s.d. l. 397). Thus the group does not simply climb up onto the stage, but also arranges itself about a table and begins to partake of the Passover feast. The contrast is thus particularly effective when the curtains of the council house unclose, revealing another convocation—an infernal council taking place simul-taneously. If the group in Simon's house simply continues quietly eating, gently reminding the audience of its presence while the council proceeds, the greatest effect is achieved. This is why it is best to have the two structures in the same general sighting plane, rather than ar-ranged side-by-side. One should be able to see both groups easily at the same time, to watch Jesus eating the Passover food, fulfilling the requirements of the Old Law, as the Jews progressively devise the tortures and death they plan to inflict on him for breaking the require-ments of that Law.

At the precise moment when the Jews realize that there must be some means devised to separate Jesus from his disciples, action begins again at the house of Simon. Thus the plan which will lead to the shedding of Christ's blood, and the rending of his body, takes shape as Christ prepares to give those tortures their eternal, saving, sacramental quality. Theatrically, the effect is striking. Originally Judas apparently went to the council of the Jews directly at the point where they ponder how to get Jesus alone. In the manuscript as it survives, however, the playwright or a reviser, whoever was responsible for this version, substituted Mary Magdalene's pouring of ointment on Christ's head, and her request for absolution from sin. In the Digby play of the life of Mary Magdalene the stage directions specify that at the moment when Jesus orders the seven devils to leave Magdalene's body: 'with this word vij dyllys shall dewoyde frome the woman, and the bad angyll enter into hell with thondyr.'[12] Whether or not this occurs here is not certain, though it is possible. Magdalene does specifically say that the seven devils have left her. In any case Mary Magdalene's recognition of the saving power of Christ leads naturally into Christ's lament that one of those seated at the table will betray him, and contrasts as well with the refusal to recognize this power on the part of the council taking place at the same time. Each disciple denies that he plans such a betrayal, with Judas the last to speak. Jesus answers his question as to whom the betrayer will be by warning Judas directly that he is a grown man, of the age of reason, and thus, by implication, fully responsible for his acts. 'Remember thiself avyse the ryght welle / Thou art of grett age and wotysst what is reson' (p. 251, ll. 588–9).

Judas' answer is to rise, enter the place, and announce his determination to betray Jesus. Such an action is clearly not part of the scriptural account, nor is the Betrayal particularly likely to have occurred in this fashion. Judas' flat opening statement that he has 'cowntyrfetyd ... a prevy treson' (p. 251, l. 590) is certainly not a bit of sophisticated characterization either. Quire P, comprising only two leaves, and containing the Betrayal, probably represents an originally separate earlier play on this subject which has been adapted to fit the Passion sequence. The playwright has kept it in pretty much its older form because he was interested at this point not in psychological realism nor historical verisimilitude but in symbolic juxtapositions. By telescoping the probable time sequence of the original events (we really don't know when or how the betrayal occurred, of course), the playwright is able to maintain the pace of the play, to achieve the illusion of events moving ahead with inexorable finality. We can never forget, in this play, the context in which the Last Supper took place. What the playwright is referring to is the double consciousness familiar to anyone who has taken part in a Maundy Thursday celebration of the Eucharist, not a psychologically believable portrait of Judas. Thus we do not even find the traditional explanation that Judas was angered at the waste of money involved in Mary Magdalene's anointing of Jesus, nor the explanation that he resented the loss of his tithe as treasurer which he would have obtained had the ointment been sold and given to the poor. Judas simply says that he is selling his master from covetousness, and displays a jolly heartiness in the transaction that squares oddly with his few speeches questioning Christ in Simon's house. The Jews proffer the thirty pieces of silver, the bargain is struck, and preparations begin for Gethsemane.

Again we have to do a bit of interpreting of the sequence of events, as the stage direction at the end of quire P is not entirely clear. Judas says (p. 253, ll. 650–1) that he must rejoin his master, and is present later during part, though not all, of the institution of the Eucharist. He must therefore retire quietly to Simon's house as the convocation in the council house breaks up. It is interesting to see that the playwright apparently felt that he did not want any visual distractions as the sequence of actions actually instituting the Eucharist were presented. After all, this is the central event in the drama of Corpus Christi. Thus, after they have discussed what preparations are needed for the capture of Christ in the garden, the Jews separate back to their different scaffolds. The stage direction reads

Here the buschopys partyn in the place and eche of hem takyn here leve þe contenawns resortyng eche man to his place with here meny to make redy to take cryst and than shal the place ther cryst is in shal sodeynly vnclose rownd abowtyn shewyng cryst syttyng at the table and his dyscypulys eche in ere degre ... (p. 254, s.d. l. 669).

Here is enough action to cover Judas' return. Apparently the playwright intended that after Judas left Simon's house the curtains there should be pulled, ending the visual contrast. One presumes that there would be some means provided for Judas to re-enter the group without being seen before the curtains opened.

Christ, while instituting the celebration of the Eucharist, follows the practice in this play of having one of the characters within the play present doctrinal instruction. Connections between the Old Law and the New are explicitly, and naturally, made. Having given a full exegesis of the Mass, Christ then proceeds to offer the bread, using the words of the Mass, to each disciple in turn. When he reaches Judas he warns him one final time, 'Judas art thou avysyd what thou shalt take?', to which Judas respònds, 'Lord thi body I wyl not forsake' (p. 257, ll. 772–3). In performance one feels a momentary catch of breath at the audacity of the words with which Judas determines his fate. Since he is determined, Jesus gives him the bread, still warning him that it will be his damnation. Christ then speaks to the group as a whole (the preceding exchange was clearly private), saying again that someone will betray him. Each denies it around the circle till the turn comes to Judas. He then asks Christ, 'Is it owth I lord', (p. 258, l. 783) to which Jesus answers, 'Judas thou seyst that word / Me thou ast solde that was thi ffrend / That thou hast begonne brenge to an ende' (p. 258, ll. 784–6). At this point a stage direction specifies that Judas should leave and 'gon ageyn to the jewys' (p. 258, s.d. l. 786). However, the direction then indicates that there is an optional speech to be spoken by the Jews if desired, or else a speech by the Demon should be used. As the speech by the Jews is missing (the Demon's speech is on the top of the first leaf of a new quire), it seems clear that the playwright or a reviser had realized that there was no point in further discussion between Judas and members of the council, which were all dispersed, but chose instead to use the demon figure from the Prologue to underscore the effect of Judas' action. Also, he clearly did not wish any contrasting action to be included during the distribution of the wine, nor the washing of the disciples' feet. Thus the final action on the scaffold stage of Simon's house is completely focussed and the central final acts of the Last Supper take place alone, without distractions. Full use had already been made of the multiple stages; here a single stage must receive the audience's full attention.

In using the structures of a place-and-scaffold stage, it is possible to make certain theological connections by using the same structure for events which reproduce the same pattern through history. Thus if there is a mountain on which Isaac is to be sacrificed, it makes good sense for the same mountain to double later as Calvary. Nevertheless, within a given sequence of scenes, each separate action really demands a new structure. One mark of the successful use of place-and-scaffold staging is whether the transitions are made without strain. The passage from the house of Simon to Mount Olivet is easily provided for. Christ simply indicates that the meal is over, and that he must walk to Bethany. Once there, he leaves the disciples in 'a place lyche to a park'

(p. 262, s.d. l. 908) as indicated earlier, asking them to watch for him while he prays. Having left them, he 'goth to olyvet and settyth hym down one his knes and prayth to his fadyr . . .' (p. 262, s.d. l. 916). Here one could use the Heaven scaffold that had been used earlier, particularly if Eden were closely associated with it, but there is no doctrinal reason for doing so. As I have suggested before, it is more likely that Olivet becomes Calvary the following day simply because mountains are not easy to construct. Here the mountain provides a good cover for the angel, and a logical place for him to retreat to once he has offered Christ the Eucharist. There seems little doubt that a separate location is indicated for this section of the Passion.

The final action is one that lends itself particularly well to the open place of the place-and-scaffold stage. Christ is just leaving the mountain when a small armed band enters the place, carrying lighted torches and cressets, and providing a striking contrast to the strained quiet of the scene on the Mount. Judas appears with this group, appropriately, to give the traitor's kiss. Before he can act, however, there is a piece of stage business inserted which establishes Christ's real majesty and presence. When Jesus asks the Jews, that is, the armed band noisily filling the place, what their business is, the sound of his voice prostrates them until he gives them leave to rise. Only then does Judas administer the kiss. Here there is no problem of restricted space; here there can be a real *mêlée* in which Peter's assault on Malchus' ear is the central action. Christ again stills the crowd, further asserting his personal power over the events that lead to his death. This calm contrasts with the frantic words of Rufin and Leon, which lead in turn to the final jostling, shouting crowd scene, full of 'gret cry and noyse' with 'some drawyng cryst forward and some bakwarde and so ledyng forth with here weponys alofte and lytys brennyng . . .' (p. 267, s.d. l. 1036).

This is very nearly the finale. As the shouting crowd fades off out of the place, the lone figure of Mary Magdalene, part of the group around Jesus since the Last Supper, detaches itself from the crowd and runs across the place to the temple, there to tell Mary the terrible news of his arrest. The play then closes with the traditional lament of the Virgin, to resume in Herod's court the following year.[13] The Virgin's question— 'Why is it necessary for God's son to suffer all this? Is this the only way to save mankind?'—is a fitting end to the play, a conclusion which brings the action to an appropriate close.

One realizes how well-adapted to the action of these events in Passion Week the place-and-scaffold stage is when one compares the

N-Town first Passion Play with one of the York plays dealing with some of the same events—the Cordwainers' play of *The Agony and the Betrayal*.[14] This play is one of the most difficult to mount on a pageant wagon in the York cycle, for it requires two separate locations as well as a large number of actors.[15] A brief review of the action in this play should indicate the limitations of the pageant wagon stage for actions as complicated as the Agony and Betrayal and offer a concluding point of contrast between the characteristic strengths of the two theatres.

The York Cordwainers' play opens in the garden. Probably some structural indication of Mount Olivet is called for, for Jesus does leave his disciples, as in the scriptural account, and withdraw to pray. As in the N-Town version, there is an angel, though this one simply speaks to Jesus words of reassurance, suggesting that he appears in the mountain structure, but that there was no room provided for more than a simple appearance. Whether more disciples are present than Peter, James, and John, all of whom have speaking parts, is doubtful. Thus one effect of the restricted space is a reduction in the size of the crowd scene in the garden through a reduction in the total number of disciples present.

At the conclusion of the Agony, when Jesus has gently rebuked Peter for his boasting, this group must freeze while the action commences in the palace at the other end of the wagon. This convention we are already familiar with, but one realizes how much more effectively contrasting actions, both visually present at once, could be handled in the place-and-scaffold theatre. Judas enters the palace (or comes out of its rear enclosed area), where the plot is quickly hatched. Four soldiers, with four of the Jews and Malchus, are dispatched to take Jesus, led by Judas. They could conceivably descend to the street, but this seems unlikely. Furthermore despite the well-known stage direction from Coventry calling for Herod to rage both in the street and on the pageant, action on the wagon stage is generally contained within its own spatial frame, unless there is a specific need for that frame to be extended to include the audience directly. So here the actors in the palace move slowly across the small central open playing area. After all, there is only a two-line speech by Jesus to cover the cross between the two locations. Where in the N-Town play Jesus' words alone flattened his attackers, here several references to the power of the light shining from him suggest that some visual theatrical effect was aimed at. A more important difference, however, lies in the fact that only Malchus steps forward when Jesus is fully identified. Thus instead of a general scuffle, in which he is the one hurt, here he alone is attacked by Peter alone. This solves the space problem, but it would not be particularly arresting as theatre. Nor is there any indication in the dialogue (stage directions are entirely absent from this play) that anything more than the simplest confrontation scene precedes Jesus' capture, which ends the play. In short, the action is limited to a few restricted gestures, and a large amount of posturing.

One hesitates to blame the playwright of the York version for the stiff constricted quality of his play. He had relatively little choice in the arrangement of his material, and none in the form of the theatre for which it was written. Crowd scenes, particularly ones in which the crowd engages in considerable action, simply do not translate any better onto a pageant wagon stage than the battles of *Henry IV* or *Henry V* translated on to the stage of the Globe. Nevertheless it was not incumbent on the York playwright to include every part of the original narrative. Nor, for that matter, is the scene in the palace even based on scripture. Where the choice made is for a self-contained, coherent single dramatic incident, the wagon stage comes into its own. On the other hand, an action with a number of locations and a large cast need not be a success in the place-and-scaffold stage. There movement between locations must be motivated, and action involving multiple playing areas must seem to require a more extended sphere of action. The success of the first N-Town Passion Play arises as much from the pace of the action, the use of contrasting playing areas to develop simultaneous, interlocking actions, as from the playwright's handling of crowd scenes.

Determining the relative excellence of a particular medieval play requires, then, consideration of the adaptation made to the theatre for which the play was written. In such a study, generic terms, 'Corpus Christi cycle play', or 'morality play', are of little or no help. Rather than comparing the play under scrutiny with plays of similar theme or content, we must compare them with other plays written for place-and-scaffold, station-to-station, or booth stage theatres. For example, *The Second Shepherd's Play* of the Wakefield cycle, perhaps the most frequently anthologized medieval play next to *Everyman*, can be understood best as a play written for the focussed confines of the pageant wagon stage. There the visual juxtaposition of the two births gains from proximity. The transformation of the *pastores* into pastors under the influence of the good news takes place on the neutral ground between the house of Mak and the Manger, the setting earlier in the play for the worldly quarrels of those same shepherds. We have come to see that the play is hardly blasphemous in the juxtaposition of the two worlds, a juxtaposition so often found on the restricted stage of the pageant wagon. Here then is a supreme example of a playwright who could take his conventions and adapt them perfectly to his vision, conventions we do well to keep firmly in mind as we analyse the play.

Yet there is clearly more to a play than its staging. We return to the great plays of the Elizabethan theatre as much for the insights that they give into human character as for the physical theatrical effects created within the conventions of the playhouses of London. So too the characters in medieval English drama hold our attention when properly understood. It is to these—the people who strut their brief moments on the medieval stages that we have attempted to recapture—that our attention must now turn.

4

CHARACTER AND VERISIMILITUDE

In any discussion of the strengths and weaknesses of medieval English drama a sure sign of strength has generally been felt to be the inclusion of realistic detail. This use of realistic detail is seen as a good in itself, irrespective of the use to which it is put. Yet we have already found in discussing such matters as stage structures that excellent drama does not necessarily require an accurate re-creation of such settings as the manger in Bethlehem. Nor is the juxtaposition of the council of the Jews and the house of Simon in the N-Town enactment of the Last Supper, a play we have found on other grounds to be of superior quality, in any way to be considered a faithful rendering of the real conditions in which the Last Supper took place. It is true that the York *Nativity* was cited earlier as impressing a modern audience with the specific reality of Christ's human birth. At the same time it should be recognized that it is not the fact of the birth that usually receives the appellation 'realistic', but rather the somewhat gross examination of the Virgin by Salome, the midwife, to ascertain whether or not she is still a virgin after giving birth to Jesus.

The fact of the matter is that the term realistic is not usually employed to describe the physical settings for the plays, which until recently were regarded as crude and amateurish work. Rather the term 'realism' is most often used to describe the comic or violent elements in medieval drama, particularly as they appear in such characters as Noah's shrewish wife or the irreverent Cain.[1] When it appears, the term 'realism' is used without definition, the reader, it is assumed, sharing the critic's own sense of what it means. What is assumed is the meaning given to the term by the school of French Realists of the later nineteenth century, writers such as Flaubert and Zola, and in drama particularly by such plays as Ibsen's *Ghosts*.[2] For such writers realism represented a break with the idealism of the Romantic era, and is characterized by an insistence that the writer's task was to record the data of sense impressions, verifiable in common experience, as the only reality which can be known.[3] Writers in the movement known as Realism denied the possibility of describing, let alone knowing, the supposed world of ideal forms. Their revolt against idealism led such writers as Zola to describe the ugly insanity of mob behaviour, or death by starvation in a mine disaster, and Ibsen to base a play on the long-term effects of syphilis. As it happened, the Realist school of literature appeared at the same time as Darwin's *Origin of Species* in 1859, and throughout its history 'Realism' has been associated with theories of human development which stress the effect on mankind of implacable laws of this world, whether of Nature or society, as opposed to literature which adheres to a belief in the operation of the laws of a transcendent God.[4]

No work of medieval literature belongs to this school of writing. Chaucer may relate for us the specific details of a human love affair, to the point of noting Pandarus' departure for a cushion at the crucial juncture of Troilus' first night with Cressida; but the total effect of his work is to insist on the impermanence of human affection when compared to the eternal love of God. No writer of medieval drama, including the so-called York 'Realist', is concerned to reproduce the concrete details of medieval life, pleasant or unpleasant, as the only commonly shared area of experience knowable to his audience and himself. For every writer of the plays with which we are concerned, eternity is that reality against which every human action must be judged; an eternity in which the individual's specific acts will place him either with the blessed or the damned. In order to reserve the term 'realism' for its proper period in literary history, therefore, let us follow the suggestion of Edwin H. Cady, who, writing on the subject of realism in American fiction, proposed that the term 'realism' should not be used to describe 'local, partial, even fragmentary uses of realistic effects to contribute to what will in the long run and total effect be unrealistic'. For such effects he would propose the term 'verisimilitude', reserving 'realism' for works whose total effect is to insist on the data of common-sense experience as the only subject capable of being described.[5] In assessing the strengths and weaknesses of character portrayal in medieval drama our concern must be to determine what ends the dramatist employs his realistic details to serve—rather than, as in the past, simply noting with approval their existence, and moving on.[6]

Any discussion of early English drama which concentrates upon characters whose actions and speech are close to the patterns of normal human behaviour and whose actions are at the same time either comic or vicious (the normal indices used to identify realism) must first reckon with the influential conception of the double tone of Gothic drama proposed some twenty years ago by A. P. Rossiter. Rossiter subscribed to the evolutionary theory of the development of early English drama, particularly as it sought to account for the shift in locale from the cathedral to the streets. The gradual intrusion of undisciplined elements of comedy was supposed to have been the best index of the progressive 'secularization' of the drama. In *English Drama from Early Times to the Elizabethans*, Rossiter averred that 'The simplest explanation of the "exit" from the church is that the secular world gave room for developments which were already pressing on inventive "literary" minds'.[7] These developments he spelled out at some length in his chapter on 'Gothic Drama',—drama he characterized as marked particularly by a 'disturbing doubleness of tone' caused by the simultaneous inclusion of scenes of deep reverence and of biting, satirical comedy. The 'fiendish' torturers of the crucifixion plays are 'heartless comedians at the same time'.[8]

Rossiter based his theory of the Gothic 'double tone' on the rituals of a medieval church which could simultaneously include both the celebration of the Nativity (and the death and resurrection of its god) and a parody of these celebrations in the Feast of Fools. Having found this ambivalence not only in the late medieval drama of England, but also in the fifteenth-century paintings of Breughel and Bosch, Rossiter concluded that

We are left to wrestle with the uncombinable antinomies of the medieval mind: for these immiscible juxtapositions constantly imply two contradictory schemes of values, two diverse spirits; one standing for reverence, nobility, pathos, sympathy; the other for mockery, blasphemy, baseness, meanness or spite, *Schadenfreude*, and derision. Above all, it is the fact that the 'other spirit' is *comic* that compels reflection and analysis; for the evaluated effect of the ambivalence reaches out towards a searching irony.[9]

Rossiter himself never referred to this harsh, satiric comedy of the second tone as realistic, as he himself was concerned to establish that tone as one aspect of the ritual quality of the early drama. Ritual and realism are not synonymous, if the term realism is used in the sense we have already defined. Nevertheless he was at pains to insist upon the specific humanity of Christ's leering torturers and executioners. No discussion of the dramatic function of verisimilitude, particularly comic or violent verisimilitude, therefore, is possible if Rossiter is correct. 'Uncombinable antinomies' do not lead to a resolved synthesis on a higher order of being in the theatre, however much the critic may seek to rationalize such oppositions after the fact. For the theatre works on an immediate audience, who seldom have opportunity to reflect on the meaning of a play at leisure. If the conflict between deep religious feeling and the verisimilitude of satire cannot be resolved as the play's action unfolds, subsequent scholarly attempts to discover that resolution will be of little account.

A good test case to use in assessing the validity of Rossiter's argument is the play in the N-Town cycle entitled in the manuscript the *pagetum de purgacione Marie et joseph*, and by its editor, *The Trial of Joseph and Mary*.[10] Rossiter cited this play as a deplorable example of 'the *contemporaneity* which marks the medieval drama', for he felt that 'the placing of Joseph and Mary in a context of bribery and suspected fornication' was a demeaning offence to their dignity. Though he recognized that the pathos of Mary's plight was obvious, he strongly objected to the fact that the play 'is managed in the tone of a tragical farce of the servant-girl who has slipped up, and who is bullied and nagged with every shaming comment and indecent inquisition'.[11] Whether or not this is the correct response either in the fifteenth century or now is questionable.[12] Certainly it was not the response of a modern audience to a production of the play presented at the Ohio State University recently. Let us therefore examine the play more closely to determine precisely how the dramatist made use of verisimilitude to construct his play.

As it happens, the play is an excellent one to study in isolation, for it stands alone in the manuscript of the N-Town cycle.[13] The stage directions indicate that the play was apparently written for the focussed wagon stage described above in Chapter 2. The sources, the apocryphal *Protoevangelium of James* (a second-century Greek tract glorifying Mary's virginity) and the *Gospel of Pseudo-Matthew* were freely adapted by the play's composer, particularly in the addition of such details as the character of the gross, 'realistic' Summoner, the primary source of Rossiter's discontent.

To begin with, the plot of the play hardly depends on the audience's

sense of a common level of experience. Mary and Joseph are haled
before an ecclesiastical court and subjected to a trial by ordeal to prove
Mary's innocence. The ordeal derives from the Old Testament, and
consists of drinking a purgative potion.[14] If the accused is guilty of the
purported sin, his or her face will become blotched. Needless to say,
both Joseph and Mary pass the ordeal without a trace of sin. Such a
trial apparently never took place in the history of English trials by
ordeal, and is based not on actual practice but on the 'bitter water'
ordeal of Numbers v, 11 ff.[15] Thus the actual events of the play partake
more of the fabulous world of the *Vitae Patrum*, where extraordinary
miracles were a daily occurrence, than the world of fifteenth-century
England.

What gives this play its particular and undisputed strength is the fact
that the playwright saw in it an opportunity to go one step beyond the
plays treating of *Joseph's Return*, where Joseph's own reaction to Mary's
undoubted pregnancy is dramatized, to present in highly concrete terms
the reaction of others on learning the same news. Modern readers who
are offended by the medieval world's excessive interest in the facts of
Mary's pregnancy might reflect that the Virgin Birth is in many ways
a more difficult article of faith to accept than the Resurrection. It is to
the credit of medieval writers that they faced that necessity of belief
squarely, and insisted on the factual reality of that article of faith whatever one's individual feelings might be. In the case of *The Trial of
Joseph and Mary* the playwright offers his audience the opportunity to
identify with the responses of one of four different levels of society,
all reacting differently to the fact of Mary's pregnancy, and, through
vicarious participation in the rectification of those responses, the
opportunity to arrive at an appropriate belief in the reality of Mary's
virginity.

The first level of response is that of the Summoner, Den. His opening
speech, a direct address to the audience, has generally been taken as a
singular example of the medieval emphasis on the contemporary, and is
thus cited as part of his realistic characterization. Den summons a
whole list of characters with Middle English names to the bishop's
court. Furthermore, those summoned are supposedly members of the
audience. In point of fact this opening is frankly and avowedly theatrical, and has little to do with his particular response to the Virgin's
pregnancy. As Professor Kolve points out in his seminal chapter on
'The Drama as Play and Game' the medieval audience was never
allowed to become confused as to the nature of the scene portrayed.

Figures such as *Contemplacio*, who ends the play on *The Visit to Eliza-beth*, insist on the nature of the theatrical experience as other, removed from the actual world of the audience—a world, in fact, of game.[16] Den, by calling attention to the fact that the audience exists with his opening 'A-voyd Serys', reminds the audience that they are watching a play. At the same time, of course, the list of English names insists that the play that is to follow will be concerned with the eternal patterns of human response. Den's own response is that of the servant of the law who has lived so long in the world of human corruption that he cannot conceive of any but the basest motives. Recent screen portrayals of the 'tough cop' in action remind us of the permanence of this attitude. Thus when he is later sent with the summons for Mary and Joseph to appear in court, he treats them exactly as he would any other of his victims. He is portrayed as a petty tyrant who uses his power to exact deference, for in his cross from the bishop's seat to the location where Mary and Joseph are standing, he bullies the audience:

> Do me sum wurchep befor my face
> Or be my trowth I shal yow make
> If that I rolle yow up in my race
> Ffore fere I shal do your ars qwake.   (ll. 121-4)

If he is crossing through the audience, this language would have even more impact. But it is, again, language which insists on the theatrical experience in progress. The actual verisimilitude comes into play when he accosts Joseph in the terms that gave Rossiter so much pain:

> A Joseph good day with thi ffayr spowse.
> My lorde the buschop hath for yow sent
> It is hym tolde that in thin house
> A cuckolde is bowe is eche nyght bent.   (ll. 129-32)

He then turns to Mary with the question

> Ffayre mayde that tale ye kan best telle.
> Now be youre trowthe telle your entent
> Dede not the Archere plese yow ryght welle?   (ll. 134-6)

When both parties protest their innocence, in calm and dignified terms, Den, realizing that there is no possibility of obtaining a bribe to buy him off, orders them to follow him adding with heavy sarcasm that

---

rolle ... up enroll   *in my race* on my (hurried) trip
cuckolde is bowe cuckold's bow

Mary must be a 'clene huswyff' if she says so, but that if his wife ever presented him with 'suche a pak', he would know how to treat her.

Here the verisimilitude derives from the fact that Den has never heard of either of these people before. To him, they are just one more example of the ancient problem of old men with young wives. The theme of January and May was worn threadbare in medieval anti-feminist literature, but it did not therefore lose its currency. One need only turn to the comedies of the Restoration to find the same theme in heavy use. The theme is both conventional, in a literary sense, and realistic, in that in an age of arranged marriages, such pairings did in fact occur with sufficient frequency for the results to be common knowledge. Given, therefore, Den's background and Mary's condition, his reaction is thoroughly understandable.

The attitude of the two 'detractors' who follow Den on stage at the beginning of the play is another matter. Both of them identify themselves by the generic and unrealistic names of Backbiter and Raise Slander in the manner of morality vices on their first entrance. Their opening remarks, again a theatrical convention rather than an attempt at realistic characterization, consist of direct address to the audience, spelling out exactly what sort of vice they represent.[17] For example the second detractor, having been asked by his fellow to identify himself for the benefit of 'alle these pepyl', answers 'I am bakbytere that spyllyth alle game / bothe kyd and knowyn in many a place' (ll. 29–30). Again the language of this opening insists on the identity of the audience as audience, and the actors as taking part in a play, exactly as did Den's opening prologue.

Once this introduction is past, however, the characterization of the two detractors begins rapidly to acquire the specific qualities of small-town gossips. When asked for any juicy tidbits of news that he might have, Raise Slander establishes the play's context with economy, placing Mary precisely within a category of the audience's experience.

> Syr in the tempyl a mayd ther was
> Calde mayd mary the trewth to telle.
> Sche semyd so holy withinne that plas
> Men seyd sche was ffedde with holy Aungelle.
> Sche made a vow with man nevyr to melle
> But to leve chast and clene virgine.
> How evyr it be, here wombe doth swelle
> And is as gret as thinne or myne. (ll. 41–8)

Every member of any audience for this play has known a girl, 'holier than thou', who has set herself up while still a young teenager as a paragon of sexual virtue, only to demonstrate on reaching maturity that she is as susceptible to the temptations of the flesh as any of the rest of us. If this play is presented in sequence with the Marian cycle, the audience will know that Mary in fact *was* fed by angels while in the temple, once she had taken her vow in public. The language of Raise Slander's summary, however, is precisely that of one who had not been present at any of those events, but who had become aware subsequently of Mary's reputation for holiness. To the inveterate gossip no morsel is so exquisite as a tale of fallen virtue which reduces a paragon to the gossip's acknowledged level of fallen humanity. And of course one realizes that if Mary in her own lifetime had had a reputation for saintliness of the type already set forth in the Marian cycle, this would in fact have been exactly the reaction of most of those hearing the story of her pregnancy for the first time.

As the two detractors move across the stage, discussing whether the cause of the fall were Joseph's lack of self-control in his marital bed (he had vowed never to touch Mary at the time of their betrothal), or whether 'sum fresche yonge galaunt' had found his way to Mary's bed, their speculations are overheard by the bishop, Abiyachar, Mary's relative. He knows nothing of Mary's condition, and regards the comments of the gossips as libel. Their response is to challenge him to see for himself. Her womb, as they have already remarked, is as great as their own. Abiyachar thus provides a third response to Mary's pregnancy, that of one of her own family. The fourth is provided by the two doctors of the law at his side, who also are inclined to take Mary's side, but are less closely involved in the results of the test that is to come. It is worth remarking that this grouping provides two balanced sets of responses, one pair sympathetic to Mary's state, the other basically vindictive. Abiyachar's first response on overhearing the slanderers is to state categorically 'Ye be acursyd so hire to defame / She that is of lyff so good and holy' (ll. 75–6). The first doctor of the law warns the detractors that if they are found to be lying, the consequences for them could be very serious.

The effect of these responses is to prevent the play from becoming the 'tragical farce of the servant-girl who has slipped up' that Rossiter took it to be. Mary's dignity is supported initially by characters within the play, characters who are drawn as 'realistically' as those delighting in Mary's supposed downfall. For example, when Mary's supporters are presented with the undoubted fact of her pregnancy, and her stout

insistence that she is still a maid, it is not surprising to find them shifting
their ground somewhat. The demurrer of the first doctor of the law to
Mary's avowal of continued virginity is based on what he knows of
human nature—'but if sum man the had ovyrlayd / Thi wombe
shulde never be so gret iwys' (ll. 183-4). The second doctor finds
himself reluctantly driven to accuse Joseph of fathering the child, giving
Backbiter his cue to present Joseph with his dilemma; either he did it,
or he must admit to being a cuckold. Within the realm of normal
human experience there can be no other conclusion, and thus Abiyachar
has no choice but to begin the ordeal.

It should be stressed that the reactions of Mary's supporters are
presented in the same terms in the sources. Both there and in the play
the high priest, or bishop, expresses a felling of betrayal at Mary's
lapse. In the *Protoevangelium of James* the high priest accosts Mary as
follows: 'Mary, why have you done this? Why have you humiliated
your soul and forgotten the Lord your God, you who were brought
up in the Holy of Holies, and received food from the hand of an angel,
and heard hymns of praise, and danced before Him? Why have you
done this.'[18] But in the sources the anger of the high priest is expressed
in full at the first confrontation. In the play, Abiyachar's first response
is more of sorrow and shame than of anger. 'Alas mary what hast
thou wrought / I am aschamyd evyn for thi sake' (ll. 169-70). When
Joseph has subsequently been cleared he addresses him with courtesy as
follows: 'Joseph with hert thank god thi lorde / Whos heygh mercy
doth the excuse' (ll. 249-50). Since Joseph is cleared, however, there
can be no question that Mary's fall is more serious than simply that of a
broken vow.

Still Abiyachar does not really lose his temper with Mary until she
has insisted again that she 'trespacyd nevyr with erthely wight' (l. 257).
To this assertion the first doctor reiterates his contention that no woman
ever got in such a predicament 'that ffrom mankynde hyre kowde
excuse' (l. 272), while the second reminds her not to tempt God's
justice. In contrast to these two speeches by those more sympathetic
to her, the two slanderers, obviously enjoying the whole scene hugely,
interject their reference to the folk belief of the Snow Child, begotten
by a snowflake which entered a woman's mouth while she slept un-
covered in a snowstorm. When, after all this, Mary still insists on her
virginity, Abiyachar finally loses his temper and vows

> Now be that good lord that alle this werd hath wrought,
> If god on the shewe ony manyr tokyn

Purgacion I trowe was nevyr so dere bowth
If I may on the in any wyse be wrokyn. (ll. 293-6)

On the concentrated space of the wagon stage Mary now begins her
ordeal. The effect of the preceding actions has been to sharpen the focus
on Mary far beyond that in the source narratives, and gradually to
isolate her from any possible source of human support. The doctors
of the law must work on the level of human experience. They can
be of no help. Joseph, exonerated, must stand helplessly aside. The
bishop, now fully engaged in the outcome, sits glowering on his
throne, waiting to exact a terrible vengeance for Mary's effrontery.
This progressive stripping away of the support of those originally
sympathetic to her is a far more real cause for the audience to identify
with Mary than any displeasure they might feel at the vulgarity of the
slanderers or Den. At the same time the audience must realize that no
human means are available to clear Mary's reputation. A miracle has
now become a necessity.

Of course on another level the audience knows that Mary must be
cleared. During the enactment of this play, however, with its quick
pace and rising action, it is possible to suspend that knowledge, to participate in the world of illusion for a moment, and to identify simultaneously with the human responses to Mary's pregnancy, and beyond
them, to Mary's plight caught in the focus of those responses. But the
moment of this realization passes quickly. If the play ended, as did the
sources, with Mary's vindication, that moment would pass too soon,
and be lost. The author of *The Trial of Joseph and Mary* had the excellent sense to take the ordeal one step further. As the ordeal supposedly
ends, and Abiyachar is expressing his astonishment at what has happened, Raise Slander offers the cynic's interpretation of what has happened—the bishop, being Mary's kin, has fixed the trial. 'The drynk is
chaungyd by sum fals wyle / That sche no shame shuld haue this steed'
(ll. 323-4). Abiyachar's response is to whirl on Raise Slander, and, because he made the first accusation, offer him the chance to test whether
the potion is harmless. Raise Slander responds that he will be glad to,
'If these two drynkerys haue not alle spent' (l. 330) (i.e., destroyed the
evidence).

The dramatic effect achieved at this point is, as I can testify from
direct experience, highly satisfying. Raise Slander suddenly falls

---

wrokyn revenged   *steed* place

writhing to the floor, his head splitting with pain. Rather than identifying with the vulgarities of the three low-life types, the audience's sympathy is now totally on Mary's side. Raise Slander's agony is received, quite frankly, with pleasure. All earlier identifications with the attitudes of Raise Slander or Backbiter have long since evaporated, if they ever existed. Instead, we as audience are treated to the enjoyable spectacle of poetic justice. However, the playwright does not long allow the audience this form of self-indulgence. Not only the agonized Raise Slander, but all the members of the bishop's court as well as the other low-life types fall to their knees to beg Mary's forgiveness. And the sin for which forgiveness is asked is that of 'cursyd langage'—defamation of character. Of this *all* have been guilty as the play has progressed. To the extent that the audience has identified with any of the four levels of response I have indicated, they too have participated in that sin.[19] They are guilty to the extent that they identify with the contrition of the players, and to the extent that they too are willing to admit having entertained doubts about the doctrine of the Virgin Birth. Members of that audience also participate in the absolution with which Mary brings the play to a close.

In the *Trial of Joseph and Mary* comic verisimilitude in no way provides one pole of an 'uncombinable antinomy' of the medieval mind. In this play there is no 'immiscible juxtaposition' between reverence and blasphemy. Nor are the comic characters the only ones who are realistically portrayed. Instead, what we find is a full range of realistic characterization, a sensitivity to the appropriate phrase delineating a particular attitude or state of mind which accurately fixes the reality portrayed. That reality consists of the eternal verities of human existence.[20] Describing the drama of the cycle plays Erich Auerbach wrote

In [this drama] all the heights and depths of human conduct and all the heights and depths of stylistic expression find their morally or aesthetically established right to exist; and hence there is no basis for a separation of the sublime from the low and everyday, for they are indissolubly connected in Christ's very life and suffering. Nor is there any basis for concern for the unities of time, place, or action, for there is but one place—the world; and but one action—man's fall and redemption.... In contrast to the feudal romance which leads away from the reality of the life of its class into a world of heroic fable and adventure, here there is a movement in the opposite direction, from distant legend and its figural interpretation into everyday contemporary reality.[21]

These words, written of the twelfth-century *Jeu d'Adam* we have already had cause to notice, are equally true of the fifteenth-century

Trial of Joseph and Mary, or of any other play making similar use of realistic character portrayal which relies on details of comic verisimilitude.

But 'realism' depended for its effects not only on the portrayal of the ridiculous as an antithesis to a Wordsworthian sublime. As noted earlier, it also insisted on the presence of violence and ugliness in the data of common experience. Because the cycle plays also include scenes of brutal violence as well as scenes of low-life comedy, earlier critics found themselves faced with what they felt to be undeniable evidences of realism, but a form of realism which offended contemporary sensibilities. Auerbach, for example, made a distinction between the realism of the early drama and its appearance in the drama of the later Middle Ages. Like Rossiter, he found the rough brutality of the Passion plays jarring and off-key. 'Later', he said, 'it is different: realism of a coarser grain begins to thrive, and varieties of mixed style, of the blunt juxtaposition of Passion and crude [crude, because brutal] farce, develop, which to us appear strange and unseemly.'[22] The height of this development Auerbach placed in the fifteenth century. Yet even though he found the farce crude, and the vulgar characters jarring, Auerbach still insisted that these elements did not represent an irreconcilable world view.[23]

It is not to our purpose to explore the reasons why at certain points in literary history artists are willing to face up to the violent strains in human nature, and to give those strains full play in their art. The recent debate on the sources of aggression in human nature is as heated as it is because of the stubborn adherence by intellectual heirs of the liberal movement to the belief that human nature is basically good, and that one need only change the conditions of existence to give that goodness its full opportunity to flower. Suggestions that original sin may include an active propensity towards violence strike at the heart of this theory of human nature. But such a debate was unthinkable in the medieval period, where humanity's eternal willingness to sin in myriad ways was taken for granted. It is certainly true that by the end of the medieval period more stress was being placed on the fact of sin than was characteristic of the writings of, say, the twelfth century. This does not mean that Bernard of Chartres was any less willing to acknowledge the brutality in human nature than for instance, the writer of the York *Crucifixion*. What concerns us as we approach the portrayal of these elements in human nature as they appear in fifteenth-century drama is not the fact that the brutality of humanity is portrayed, but whether or not that portrayal is necessary to the theme and structure of the plays in which it appears. As examples, let us examine a work of the Wakefield Master, the *Coliphizacio*, or *The Buffeting of Christ*, and the highly realistic and powerful York version of the Crucifixion.

To understand the qualities of these plays which are peculiarly their own, and not part of the well-developed body of traditions associated with the central event in Christian history, it is well to determine what form narrative events in the plays had assumed by the fifteenth century. Determination of specific sources in such cases is virtually impossible, for the variety of sources available to a writer on the Passion was considerable. For an understanding of the unique as well as the traditional qualities of the plays in question, the best approach must be through a general reading in the vernacular sources of the plays drawn on by the playwrights themselves.[24]

In the case of the *Coliphizacio*, the sources are supposedly the *Northern Passion* for the overall structure of the events as recounted in the Gospels, and the apocryphal *Gospel of Nicodemus* for some specific accusations made during the course of Christ's interrogation.[25] Certainly as opposed to such a source as *The Stanzaic Life of Christ* or the *Southern Passion* it is clear that the scene of Christ's first interrogation before Annas and Caiphas is closest to the version in the *Northern Passion*. However, a reading of the Vulgate accounts in the Gospels of Matthew (xxvi, 57–75), Mark (xiv, 53–65), Luke (xxii, 54–71), and John (xviii, 13–24) against a Gospel Harmony, for instance, that in Pepysian MS 2498, suggests that a source of this kind could just as well have been used.[26] In view of the fact that such a potential source is ignored in the most influential discussion of the *Coliphizacio*,[27] as well as the fact that we can no longer take a thorough knowledge of the Gospel accounts for granted, it seems worthwhile to include the entire account from the *Pepysian Gospel Harmony* before proceeding to a discussion of the Wakefield Master's originality in constructing his play, particularly as it relates directly to the issue of verisimilitude.

The account begins at the point where Jesus, having been seized in Gethsemane, is bound and taken to be interrogated by the chief priest, Caiphas:

And tho ladden hij Jesu to Annas hous, that hadde the bisschopes doughtter Cayphas that ilk yere ywedded. . . . [There then follows, as in the *Northern Passion*, Peter's Denial of Christ. As this is omitted in the Wakefield Cycle entirely, it is not included here.] And tho als Jesus stoode tofore Annas, hij askeden hym of his deciples and of his techynge. And he ansuered and seide that his techynge was noughth of felonye in priuete, bot al aloude tofore the folk there he preched in the temple. And on of hem gaf hym a buffet under the ere, and asked hym if he schulde so answere the bisshopp. And Jesus hym ansuered and badde if he hadde oughth mysseide, that he schulde telle hym where of; and if he ne couthe telle whereof, that he smott hym nomore. And tho soughtten hij fals witnesse upon Jesu, forto done hym to the deth. And tho comen summe and saiden upon hym, that he hadde seide that he wolde destruen Goddes temple and maken it hole agein withinne thre dayes; and summe of hem seiden other wyse, and ne acordeden nought. And many othere fals witnesses hij beren upon hym, ac hij ne myghtten nothing acorden. And tho aros up the bisschopp, and asked Jesus wharfore that he ne ansuered nought to hem that beren witnesse ageins hym. And Jesus stoode and ne ansuered noughth. And tho conjured he hym that he schulde hem tellen if he were Crist, Goddes son. And Jesus hem seide that he it was, and that hij schulden seen hym come in the blisse of God at the juggement of al the werlde. And tho bigan the bisschop to renden his clothes; and seide that Jesus hadde mysseid, and that hij ne hadden no myster nomore of wytnessynge, for whi hij it hadden alle yherd. And he asked hem what hem thoughth best to done. And hij ansuereden alle that he was worth the deth. And tho bigonnen hij that helden Jesu forto cracchen hym, and forto scornen hym, and hidden his eiyen, and smyten hym under the ere and in the nekke, and beden hym if that he were Crist that he schulde arede who it was that hym smott. And many other schames hij seiden hym. (pp. 92–3)

The sole difference of any consequence between this account and that in the *Northern Passion* derives from the fact that the compiler of the *Pepysian Gospel Harmony* dealt with the variant Gospel accounts of the locale for the interrogation by having two houses, not one:[28] in the chapter that immediately follows the above passage, Jesus is taken to the house of Caiaphas, where the remaining questions to Jesus contained in the Gospel accounts are posed.

If one now reads over the *Coliphizacio*, one sees that the entire action dramatized is here, in the earliest accounts. The only item dropped from the play is the first buffet given Jesus for failing to adopt the properly deferential tone toward the 'bishop' during the first interchange. The physical violence is reserved, instead, for the prolonged buffeting with which the play closes. No legendary material has been added. The cast has also been reduced through transferring the accusations of the false witnesses to the mouths of the interrogators and torturers themselves. Even the game of blind man's buff, or 'hot cockles',

---

ac but   *myster* need   *cracchen* scratch   *arede* prophesy

which the torturers play with the blind-folded Christ at the end of the play, is canonical.[29] Matthew's version, for example, reads, 'Then did they spit on his face, and buffeted him, and other[s] smote his face with the palms of their hands, saying, Prophecie unto us O Christ: who is he that stroke thee'.[30] In this play originality does not lie in the handling of the brutally realistic details of the action, as in the game of 'hot cockles', but in the characterization of those who participate in that action. To that characterization we must now turn.

As one reads the play, one quickly realizes that the dramatic problem that the Wakefield Master set himself was to answer the question, 'What kind of person would do to the Lord the things the Apostles assure us took place?' The play opens quickly, with the first of the two torturers driving Christ before him like an animal, exclaiming 'Do io furth, io! and trott on apase!' (l. 1, p. 78). As we hear these words, we do realize immediately what kind of person must have beaten someone as pacific as Christ. It had to be someone for whom Jesus was not a person—someone who must dehumanize his victim if that victim threatened the basic structure of belief by which the tormenter lived. The second torturer sums up the source of their anger. 'Sich wyles can thou make, / Gar the people farsake / Oure lawes, and thyne take; Thus art thou broght in blonder' (ll. 15–18). As participators or spectators in the ideological wars of the twentieth century, it should not be hard for us to appreciate the verisimilitude of such characterization. The question, however, remains 'Is it crude, is it of a "coarser grain"?' Or, one might even admit that it is coarser than the verisimilitude of the *Jeu d'Adam*, and still insist that it is dramatically effective. So it appears to me to be.

Leaving aside the figures of the torturers for a moment, however, let us concentrate on the characterization of Caiphas and Annas. As we have seen from the *Gospel Harmony*, Caiphas was the high priest and Annas his son-in-law. Caiphas was identified by John (xviii, 14) as that high priest who gave the Jews the counsel that it was better for one man to die for the people,[31] and by Matthew (xxvi, 65) as the one who rent his clothes at Jesus' acknowledgment that he was the son of God. The *Gospel Harmony* gives this detail of rending the clothes to Annas, but otherwise he is without any distinguishing characteristics either there or in the Gospels themselves.

Within the play, the interrogation proper by these two prelates

---

Gar make

begins at line 127, after the torturers have given a summary of the various accusations brought against Jesus, accusations to be found in various places in the original Gospel accounts. Caiphas begins the examination himself by asking Jesus if he has heard the accusations, and adds the outraged query 'How durst thou the call aythere emperoure or kyng?' (l. 130). However, as in the *Gospel Harmony*, 'jesus stoode and ne ansuered noughth'. That silence drives Caiphas into the traditional fury of a medieval stage tyrant: here, however, far better motivated than most such outbursts. His tirade is finally interrupted by Annas, who has remained virtually silent himself until this point. Annas, in a splendid bit of by-play, which takes place as though Jesus were not present, smoothly seeks to calm Caiphas. 'Sir,' he says, 'ye ar vexed at all, / And perauenter he shall / Hereafter pleas you. / We may bi oure law examyn hym fyrst / ' (ll. 187–90). Caiphas, however, can hardly restrain himself from whacking Jesus out of pure unrelieved frustration.

As the interchange develops, it becomes apparent that Caiphas has been characterized as a medieval bishop of the warlike strain. One can see him struggling against the restraining arm of Annas, clad in the stage regalia of a bishop of the Old Law (i.e., modified medieval bishop's robes), venting his fury in explosive outbursts. On the other hand, Annas is portrayed as a medieval canon lawyer, a particularly smooth, oily individual, one who never himself becomes ruffled. The following dialogue is typical of the whole interchange:

> *Anna.*   Sir, speke soft and styll;
>   Let vs do as the law will.
> *Cayphas.* Nay, I myself shall hym kyll,
>   And murder with knokys.
> *Anna.*   Sir, thynk ye that ye ar a man of holy kirk;
>   Ye shuld be oure techere, mekenes to wyrk. (ll. 204–9)

The irony of Annas' thrust, the obvious contempt he feels for his irrational colleague, is a splendid touch, present throughout the exchange.

The upshot of the interchange is that Annas takes over the interrogation. Where Caiphas was all threats and bluster, Annas is sweet reason. Having sensibly warned Jesus that answering as he likes is dangerous in his present circumstances, Annas then goes on to say that he, Annas, 'shall do as the law wyll, if the people ruse thee' (l. 244). Jesus, who has not spoken at all during Caiphas' bluster, quickly answers the crucial

---

mekenes to wyrk to act (with) humility   *ruse* praise

question put by Annas, namely 'Are you the Son of God?'. Jesus answers that he is, and that furthermore they will all see him coming in clouds of glory.

This is the point in Matthew's account where Caiphas tears his clothes at the blasphemy. By contrast, in the play Christ's answer does provoke Caiphas again, but only to a verbal protest. Annas virtually tells him to 'Shut up'—'Abyde, syr! / Let vs lawfully redres' (ll. 257–8)—and he subsides. However, when Annas then suggests that, after all, Jesus might repent, Caiphas blows up again, this time at the thought that if Jesus did repent he would have to be set free, spoiling all their efforts. As Caiphas puts it 'For if he rene and be whyk, we are at an end, / All sam' (ll. 265–6). He even volunteers to give Jesus the *coup de grâce* himself, on the spot. He, too, like the torturers, sees in Christ's teachings the potential collapse of his system of belief. Whereas they react by dehumanizing Christ to the point where they can casually beat him nearly senseless, Caiphas, to whom the luxury of physical violence is denied, goaded by Christ's clear spiritual superiority to his threats of violence, grows ever less able to control himself.

The release through violence is denied to Caiphas not only because as a man of Holy Church he should be an example of meekness to others, but because (again as Annas reminds him) ecclesiastical authorities cannot impose the sentence of death. Annas quotes the words of John xviii, 31—'it is not lawful for us to kill any man'.[32] The solution must have been one familiar to any member of a medieval audience used to the jurisdiction of the two courts of the Middle Ages, religious and secular; the court of the archdeacon and that of the King's Bench. Annas, who always remembers exactly where the long-laid plot is pointing, reminds Caiphas further that 'Men of temperall laws, / Thay may deme sich cause; / And so may not we' (ll. 277–9). And as Caiphas storms on toward the buffeting scene, Annas continues to insist coolly that, now that the crucial admission has been made, it is up to them to force the hand of the secular authority, in the person of Pilate. The moment when Caiphas, having swung on Jesus and missed, cries out 'He that fyrst made me clerk and taght me my lare / On bookys for to barke—the dwill gyf hym care!' (ll. 307–8) is one of the great moments of medieval drama, capturing as it does the timelessness of Caiphas' response to a frustration imposed by adherence to a code of conduct

---

rene reign   *whyk* alive   *All sam* altogether
deme judge   *barke* bark

he never chose for himself. As the moment passes, it is Annas, still fully composed, who suggests that, since Caiphas so obviously needs some release for his frustration, it is time for some diversion, and orders the torturers to beat Christ. And as the game unfolds,[33] one realizes that Annas takes as much vicarious pleasure in Christ's agony as does Caiphas. His, however, is the pleasure of a sadist, the pleasure of Caiphas that of a bully.[34]

By now it should be clear that the ability of the Wakefield Master to achieve his objective is considerable. The varying levels of response to the challenge posed by Jesus are each given a believable dimension, each anchored in the world of fallen humanity. Christ's suffering is not, as later ages would seem to have it, a matter for remote contemplation, a subject for etherealized stained-glass windows and hasty, oblique references in the devotional life of a church too prone to accept blood-less abstractions as the proper vehicles for religious sentiment. It is part of a world we have recently been brought to see again with all too horrifying clarity; a world where man's inhumanity to man is a con-stant against which the injunction of the Second Commandment to 'Love thy neighbour as thyself' too seldom prevails. When even as great a critic as Auerbach, or as perceptive an analyst of late medieval forms as Huizinga, can turn from the portraits in the *Coliphizacio* as something cruder, less refined than the purer abstractions of twelfth-century art, we realize how pervasive still are the critical assumptions formed during the Romantic period and lasting through the Victorian age. Late medieval art and literature may have taken a 'pleasure . . . in observing every detail of this spectacle [of Christ's trial before Caiphas]' which some find 'excruciatingly prolonged'.[35] However, to label such art or literature 'crude farce' says more about the critic's own failures of appreciation than it does about the nature of that art.

The appropriate test for dramatic verisimilitude is not whether it is or is not like the idealized forms of the High Gothic, or whether it represents accurately everyday medieval life. Rather the test is whether or not that verisimilitude, no matter how shocking, serves a purpose in the play one is considering. In the *Coliphizacio* men move on the stage whose gestures and language provide us with clear insights into the nature of the men who crucified Christ, and would crucify him again were the Second Coming to occur tomorrow. As such the realistic portraits must be judged to be appropriate, and to be evidence of great artistic talent. The only real question that one could raise about the verisimilitude in the *Coliphizacio* concerns not the portraits of the prelates or the torturers, but that element in the actual buffeting scene, with which the play closes, that we can certainly identify as original to the Wakefield Master—that is, the character of the torturers' servant Froward.

Referring back to the account of the buffeting in the *Harleian Gospel Harmony*, one sees no reference to any servant sent for a blindfold. The introduction of a reluctant servant who is barely civil, grudgingly carrying out orders with a great deal of saucy backchat, is not unique to this part of the corpus of plays identified with the Wakefield Master, however. Having been summoned to get the blindfold, Froward's first response is to ask whether someone else could not do the job as well. The First Torturer responds 'Now ill myght thou the! / Well had thou thi name, for thou was ever curst' (ll. 378–9), to which Froward responds

> Sir, I myght say the same to you, if I durst.
> Yit my hyer may I clame; no penny I purst.
> I haue had mekyll shame, hunger, and thurst
> In youre seruyce.   (ll. 380–3)

As A. C. Cawley remarks in his commentary on this passage, 'These lines establish Froward's relationship with Pikeharnes of Play 1, Slawpase of Play 3, and Daw of Play 4. They all have uncomplimentary nicknames, and they all complain bitterly of the treatment they receive from their masters.'[36] Just as the ordered arches of a Gothic cathedral serve as a model for God's divinely planned, hierarchical universe, so these squabbling masters and servants must represent that world turned 'upsidoun' by man's wilful selfishness and disregard for the divine plan. Froward introduces one further side to the character of the torturers. Through him we see that their nastiness has a wider field of activity than simply that of torturing Christ. The brief altercation hardly delays the action, and it provides a necessary reference to a wider world of fallen humanity beyond the confines of the play.

Space does not permit a detailed comparison between the *Coliphizacio* and the play by the so-called York Realist on the same topic, Play XXIX in the York cycle. A few points deserve to be made, however. The York Realist includes in a play which is some fifty lines shorter all of the scriptural material on the Denial of Peter omitted by the Wakefield Master, as well as such details as the first buffet we have already noted in the *Harleian Gospel Harmony*.[37] Whatever suc-

---

myght might   *the* thrive

cess he may have had in drawing effective character portraits, it is clear that he has given himself much less space to work in. The result is a much more impressionistic, less fully-developed group of characters. Caiphas and Annas may, as J. W. Robinson suggests, exchange roles as bully and restraining force.[38] It is difficult to see this as carrying much dramatic power, however, in that the roles must both be established and then exchanged in the space of just 120 lines. Having seen the York play enacted several times, I can vouch for the fact that neither prelate has enough time on stage to establish much more than the fact that both are implacable enemies of Christ. The Wakefield Master, on the other hand, devotes 207 lines to the interrogation conducted by Caiphas and Annas—barely enough time to establish a fully developed stage character, let alone establish a character and then reverse it.

As regards the problem of extraneous realistic material added by the playwright, and our assessment of whether or not a character such as Froward with his comic insubordination is justified, we have in the play by the York Realist a fairly clear example of a motif introduced for the sake of establishing a realistic context which appears to have no further use in the play. I refer here to the bedding-down scene, in which Caiphas bids his court good night after cheerfully donning a prof- fered nightcap. This motif, like the motif of the surly servant in the work of the Wakefield Master, is apparently one that the York Realist found to his liking, for a similar bedding-down scene occurs in the two plays that follow.[39] But whereas in the *Coliphizacio* Froward serves to establish a pattern of human relationships which bears on the nature of the men who tortured Christ, and thereby contributes a further answer to the central problem posed by the action of the play, the best that can be said for the bedding-down scene in the York cycle is that it is a realistic detail used to establish the fact that it is night. This is not enough; it is comic verisimilitude for its own sake. Furthermore, the verisimilitude of the bedding-down scene is in sharp contrast to the conventional opening of the play. Where the *Coliphizacio* opens with the figure of Jesus stumbling on stage, bound, driven like an animal by two brutal torturers, Caiphas opens the York version with the con- ventional rant of a stage villain in which he, among other things, states that he knows of a particular 'karle' who refuses to acknowledge his authority. Furthermore, 'I haue sente for that segge halfe for hethyng'.[40] When asked for his reason for doing so, Caiphas lays out the charges

---

segge man   *halfe for hethyng* on account of his derision

against Jesus with which we are familiar, concluding with the statement that 'Oure knyghtis thai are furth wente / To take hym with a traye' (ll. 59–60). To have him then agree to go to bed, and to do so after drinking off a cup of wine about whose qualities we are told a good deal by one of the knights, can hardly be called tightly constructed dramaturgy. If Caiphas is holding court in his hall, as he says he is in his blustering speech, awaiting the imminent arrival of a culprit he has specifically set a trap for, it is scarcely an example of effective verisimilitude to have him suddenly leave his hall and go off to bed. His departure is in fact necessary to provide a clear stage for Peter's denial which follows immediately, and which the Wakefield Master chose to cut; but it is hardly an effective piece of stage realism. If anything it is an example of intrusive comedy for its own sake, the type of comic verisimilitude against which Eleanor Prosser raised so well deserved an objection.[41]

The same objections cannot be brought against the play in the York cycle which is not by the York Realist but which may be, for a modern audience, the most starkly realistic of the whole cycle; namely Play XXV, the *Crucifixio Christi*. This play has not normally been staged as originally intended in the triennial productions at York of the past two decades, initially because the cathedral authorities felt that it was too much for a modern audience to take, later because it was felt that it was too difficult to enact the actual raising of the cross in a properly reverent fashion. Margaret Birkett, whose production of the N-Town cycle at Grantham in 1966 was singularly effective in realizing the theatrical power of that cycle's scourging scenes, nevertheless balked at staging the Crucifixion itself, faking it behind the same wall of banners as employed at York. Not until the production of the Cornish cycle in 1969 did I see a properly executed *Crucifixion* staged in the twentieth century, though by that time the company at the University of Toronto had produced the York *Crucifixion* as it was written. I mention all this because the attitudes involved, which prevented good directors with considerable theatrical sense from staging the *Crucifixion* until the end of the '60s, are precisely those attitudes which have hampered literary criticism of the plays as well. The details of the event are too horrible to dwell on, we are told.[42] The question we must finally decide when discussing the whole issue of verisimilitude is whether a portrayal of such an event as the crucifixion of Christ which seeks to give that event an

---

traye trick

immediacy, a shocking reality, which makes one say, 'Yes, that must have been the way it was', can do so without necessarily portraying the human brutality indispensable to our sense of atrocity.

First let us be clear as to the conventional, the traditional in the play. Rossiter was correct to find analogues in painted representations of the Crucifixion, but before one marvels at the pictorial verisimilitude in the works of the Van Eycks, Breughel, or Bosch, one must understand that they, as well as the York playwright, were working within a highly developed set of conventions. For those interested in how the traditions associated with the Crucifixion developed, no more informative study can be recommended than ch. 4, entitled simply 'The Crucifixion' in F. P. Pickering's provocative *Literature and Art in the Middle Ages*.[43] Stated as briefly as possible, Pickering demonstrates in what appears conclusive fashion that every detail in medieval art depicting the *Crucifixion*—narratives, meditations, paintings, or drama —derived from attempts to expand on the simple biblical statement *crucifixerunt* ('they crucified him') in terms of prophetic statements in the Old Testament.[44] As a result of the study of the prophetic sayings two major literary traditions developed concerning the form in which the Crucifixion took place, neither of which can be related in any way to the actual forms of execution in use in Roman times.[45] To no one in the medieval period was the historical crucifixion in any way a familiar reality, a part of common everyday experience verifiable by one's senses; on a par, say, even with the realistic details of the detractors in the *Trial of Joseph and Mary* or the *Coliphizacio*. Only one of these traditions, that of the Crucifixion *jacente cruce*, where Jesus is nailed to the cross while it is laid flat on the ground, is found in the drama.[46] Within that tradition those details which strike the modern audience with particular force as representing highly original theatrical solutions to difficult problems of staging (such as the use of ropes as well as nails to fasten Christ's hands to the cross)—all these details are found to derive from a received tradition, and are in no way original to the drama. Specifically, the torturers' references to the breaking joints and sinews as the ropes are pulled, as well as the assurances that the jarring effect of the cross as it falls into place also breaks Christ's bones—all are found to be amplifications of a passage from the Psalm for Good Friday (Psalm xxi, 18): 'They have digged my handes and my feete: they have numbered al my bones.'[47] The holes drilled too far apart, the shape of the nails, as well as the ropes themselves derive from interpretations of a passage in the Easter Psalm (Psalm lvi, 9): 'Arise my

glorie, arise psalter and harp: I wil arise early'—where Christ in his
Passion is likened to the harp and psaltery of David![48]

If these shocking details are in fact all conventional, where then is the
strikingly original 'realism' of the dramatist? For we must remember,
again, that it was in their portrayal of the shocking details of common
experience that the nineteenth-century Realists were furthest removed
from the writers who had preceded them. More even than the comedy
does the violence of medieval drama appeal to the critic whose standard
of what is good has been set by Ibsen. The answer must be, once again,
in the depiction of character. As with all the successful plays, the York
Crucifixion opens quickly. The four soldiers assigned to carry out the
crucifixion are alone with Jesus on the wagon stage. The soldiers
establish quickly where they are, on Calvary, and what they are there
for, to carry out the orders of their superiors concerning a condemned
felon named Jesus. Where the buffeters were malignant, however,
these soldiers are much more detached, much more matter-of-fact.
Since Jesus 'must be dede nedelyngis by none', as one of them points
out, 'Than is goode tyme that we begynne' answers another.[49] The
rapid-fire dialogue is almost antiphonal, as each soldier speaks a one-
or two-line speech, almost in every case a rather objective, unemo-
tional comment on what is at hand. Like good workmen, they check
to make sure their tools are all there, and that the cross is ready before
they begin; only when that is settled do they address Jesus in the second
person, ordering him, 'Thou cursyd knave', to move over to the cross
so that they can get on with the job.

At this point Jesus delivers one of the only two speeches he has in
the whole play. Both are much longer than the speeches of the soldiers,
and both have a decided lyrical quality. As they are delivered, the
rough, quick-flowing movement of the play's language is broken, and
a sudden quiet descends on the action. Christ, addressing God, underlines the fact that he is about to die 'For Adam plyght for to be pyned. /
Here to ded I obblisshe me / Fro that synne for to saue mankynde'
(ll. 52–4). Furthermore, Jesus prays to God that mankind 'for me may
fauoure fynde' (l. 56) as well salvation from the fiend of Hell. To this
prayer the soldiers' response is total incomprehension. What is this
man doing praying for 'Adamkynde' when his mind ought to be on
his own situation, on the 'wikkid werkis that thou haste wrought'
(l. 66)? And as Christ obediently lays his body on the cross at their

---

nedelyngis necessarily   *pyned* tortured

bidding, one realizes that these are exactly the people Christ is dying to save.

Once Christ is prostrate, the soldiers cease to address him directly, dropping back into the third person. They agree which of the four corners of the cross each is to take (the First Soldier, at Christ's head, appears to be in charge of the detail) and then get on with the work. The dialogue leading up to the discovery that the holes are bored incorrectly, necessitating the use of cords, moves quickly, and enables one to follow exactly what is going on onstage whether or not one can actually see Jesus prostrate on the cross.[50] The soldier with Christ's right hand drives home his nail first with the satisfied comment

> Yis, here is a stubbe will stiffely stande,
> Thurgh bones and senous it schall be soght.
> This werke is well, I will warande. (ll. 102–4)

The First Soldier then sees that something is wrong, and the Third Soldier agrees. Someone did not measure correctly, and the hole is about a foot too far from the hand. The leader then proposes the use of a cord, and helps to haul the arm out so that the Third Soldier can drive in the nail. When the Fourth Soldier finds the hole for the feet bored wrongly as well, the First Soldier again reminds him that the solution is to pull Jesus' legs down into place. And as the legs are drawn down, the language adjusts to that of men hard at work, short of breath

> *i Mil.* Feste on thanne faste that all be fytte,
> It is no force howe felle he feele.
> *ii Mil.* Lugge on ye both a litill yitt.
> *iii Mil.* I schalle nought sese, as I haue seele.
> *iv. Mil.* And I schall fonde hym for to hitte.
> *ii. Mil.* Owe, hayll!
> *iv. Mil.* Hoo nowe, I halde it wele.
> *i. Mil.* Haue done, dryue in that nayle,
> So that no faute be foune. (ll. 135–42)

As they finish that part of the job, they stand back and look down at a job well done, with the additional comments, recalling Psalm xxi, that they certainly must have broken 'both synnous and veynis', *dinumerauerunt omnia ossa mea.*

The horror, I repeat, derives from the absolutely objective, uninvolved attitude expressed by the language of the soldiers. Rossiter felt

---

stubbe a short thick nail   *seele* soul   *fonde* try

that this expressed a 'fiendish delight in the inflicting of savage pain'.[51]
I, however, find no evidence of fiendish delight in this language, for
to express such feelings one must become emotionally involved with
the plight of one's victim. What these men are involved in is not
Christ's pain, but getting on with the job. If he happens to suffer more
because of the way the holes are bored, so much the worse for him.
The only emotion expressed is satisfaction that the man they have been
given to fasten to a cross is fastened down to stay.

What breaks this mood of calm objectivity is not Christ's suffering,
but the necessity of raising the cross. Extended analysis is not necessary
here, for the movement of the language is easy to follow as one reads
through the one hundred lines which cover the raising of the cross.
Suffice it to say that the language given the soldiers accords perfectly
with the action they must perform, providing a continuing realistic
dialogue of the sort we have already noted. On the first effort the
cross is too heavy, which leads to the shouting and angry recrimination
one is familiar with whenever one has to move a heavy object in
concert with others. One of the Toronto actors who played a soldier's
part reported that the cross required to support a grown man, plus the
weight of that man, is a terribly heavy burden. The weight, furthermore, is located off-centre, high on the upright, making it doubly
difficult to raise, particularly when it is done, as it is in the York
Crucifixion, by four men alone, without steadying ropes. It is almost
certain that one cannot get it up at the first try, he reported, for one
needs to get the feel of it by a trial effort. This is where the verisimilitude of the York *Crucifixion* is centred; here, in the real difficulties
associated with raising the cross. The language also provides a kind of
flow that makes it easy to *ad lib*. if the job in fact takes longer than the
written dialogue allows. Even if the cross should be dropped, as Mrs
Birkett, with good reason, feared it might be at Grantham, the language
provides a context in which such an event can be contained. It is not a
matter of maintaining a reverential tone, for the language is not concerned with reverence. It is concerned only with the mechanics of the
job, even to the necessity for wedging the base of the cross once it is
in the mortise. As with the mast of a boat, one cannot get it into a
hole where the fit is snug unless it is positioned exactly over the hole,
an almost impossible task where the weight is so high on the beam.
Thus, once the cross has finally dropped into place, the soldiers bang
home the wedges so that it will stand 'full stabely'.

At this point, with the raising complete, Christ speaks once more.

Such a spectacle as public punishment must draw an audience. Executions did for centuries, and certainly did so in the Middle Ages. And there is one here as well, the audience who has come to see the play. Over the heads of the soldiers Christ speaks out to that audience.

> Al men that walkis by waye or strete,
> Takes tente ye schalle no trauayle tyne,
> Byholdes myn heede, myn handis, and my feete,
> And fully feele nowe or ye fyne,
> Yf any mournyng may be meete
> Or myscheue mesured unto myne.
> My Fadir, that alle bales may bete,
> Forgiffis thes men that does me pyne.
> What thai wirke wotte thai noght,
> Therfore my Fadir I craue
> Latte nauere ther synnys be sought,
> But see ther saules to saue.   (ll. 253–64)

'Father, forgive them, for they know not what they do.' As the play ends, the soldiers' same blank incomprehension is maintained up to and through casting lots for Christ's robe. But that audience who has come to watch has been given a chance to see, and to realize, as medieval preachers, art, and literature all reiterated time and time again, that if Christ can forgive even those who crucified him in their ignorance, he can equally well forgive the sins of their counterparts in whatever age they may be born.

The verisimilitude we have examined in the plays above is indeed typical of the cultural life of the late Middle Ages. Huizinga devotes page after page to an analysis of the forms in which it appeared, from Claus Sluter's Well of Jacob to the birds and flowers of manuscript marginalia. Modern reproductions of the marvellous paintings of the Master of Limbourg have made this use of realistic detail more widely known than ever before. The drama of the fifteenth and early sixteenth centuries in England was part of the artistic movement which took a general interest in the specifics of this world, following the philosophical shift from Realism (the medieval form of Idealism) to Nominalism.[52] The appearance of verisimilitude, comic or otherwise, in the cycle drama cannot, therefore, be noted as a particular virtue of that art form, nor is the presence or absence of verisimilitude an index of a playwright's skill. Rather, precisely as we found in the case of various staging

---

tyne lose *fyne* end   *bales may bete* ills may ease

devices, it is the use to which a playwright puts that verisimilitude, particularly in the depiction of character, that should be of interest. From the plays that we have examined it should be clear that some of those uses could be highly effective. Indeed, here, in the realistic character portrayals of the civic cycle drama, is the area in which one must look for the techniques of effective dramatic character portrayal inherited by the dramatists of the later sixteenth century.

The plays of the travelling troupes posed other problems, and constitute another tradition to which we must now turn.

5

MORALITY AND FARCE

The bulk of our discussion thus far has concentrated on the civic religious drama of late medieval England. Pervasive though it was, reaching down from the great cathedral cities to the smallest villages within the county and lasting well into the sixteenth century, up until the middle or later reign of Queen Elizabeth, this drama nevertheless does not encompass the whole range of late medieval dramatic activity in England. But if establishing the context for the civic religious cycle drama is difficult, establishing the contexts for the other forms of dramatic activity which developed at the same time is even more a matter of guesswork. Some of the problems have already been alluded to in Chapter 1. To that drama, and to those problems we now must turn.

One distinction drawn between the civic religious drama and those other major forms which survive is to label the civic drama as 'amateur', and that of the small travelling groups of players who begin to appear in the late fourteenth century as 'professional'. This is the distinction drawn, for example, by Glynne Wickham in his discussion of 'Amateur and Professional Acting in the Middle Ages'.[1] The distinction is valuable if by 'amateur' we do not mean 'amateurish'. Records of the great cities such as Coventry and York firmly establish the concern that civic authorities had to ensure that acting for civic drama was of as high a quality as possible. Yet however well they acted, however much they may have carried their town drama abroad, civic players did not depend primarily on their acting for their bread. Nor does the surviving evidence suggest that their tours were of long duration. By contrast, records from the late fourteenth and fifteenth centuries testify to the emergence of groups of actors performing plays in the towns of England as a means of making a living. These actors, and their plays, developed in ways quite separate from the civic religious drama of late medieval England, though the two appeared at about the same time, and did influence each other as they developed.

When one talks of travelling players, and of the appearance of payments to them in late medieval records, one must proceed with some caution, for one is faced immediately with a terminological problem. Throughout the fourteenth century, records such as those of Durham Priory note payments to a host of performers—*mimi*, *ministralli*, *histriones*, *lusores*, or *ludatores*. The terms were, however, not interchangeable. Modern derivatives of *histrio*, for example, tempt us to gloss that term as 'actor' and to see it as equivalent to the terms *lusor* or *ludator*. Wickham thus posits the payments made at Shrewsbury in 1483 to *sex histrionibus domini Regis* as being made to the same group noted in the accounts of Selby Abbey for 1479, the *histrionibus ducis Gloucestriae*.[2] Yet from a careful study of the records of payments to various classes of entertainers in Kent, Giles Dawson concluded that the terms *mimi*, *ministralli*, and *histriones* are all synonyms for what we now refer to as 'minstrels', and that the scribes at least in that county used only the terms *lusores*, *ludatores*, and *homines ludentes* to describe that other class of entertainer we now call 'players', meaning 'actors'.[3] My own study of the records of Lincolnshire and the town of King's Lynn bears out this distinction in usage. Since it is usually held that minstrels had little to do with acting,[4] this terminological distinction would mean that the *histriones* at Shrewsbury cannot be counted as players.

If, however, *histrio* is a synonym for minstrel, and if at the same time Thomas de Cobham's categories of *histrio* can be applied equally well to the entire group of minstrels—those who entertain by transforming their bodies with 'lewd' leaps and gestures, either naked or wearing horrible masks; those who follow the courts of the great and tell libels and scurrilous tales of those who are absent; and those who play musical instruments, either singers at feasts performing lascivious songs, or the *ioculatores* who sing songs of the great and of the saints[5]—then the lines drawn between the minstrels and the first *lusores* or *ludatores*, who are consistently associated with dramatic presentations, may not be all that sharp. For one thing, English actors well into the Elizabethan period were noted for their dexterity in performing acrobatic feats. Tarlton and Will Kempe preserved, in the character of the clown, many other ancient theatrical traditions of the minstrel troupes.

Rather than insist that minstrels had nothing to do with players, I am inclined to believe that the development was much more likely to have been that proposed by Glynne Wickham.[6]

As a defence against the attacks of clerics such as Cobham, Professor Wickham proposes that medieval minstrels, whatever their speciality, attained respectability and a measure of protection by banding together in troupes under the leadership of a socially respectable *trouvère*, Cobham's *ioculator*, the descendant of the Anglo-Saxon *scop*. If we think of this troupe as containing within itself the talents of a group of vaudeville artists, we are probably closer to the truth of the matter than if we think of them as exclusively musicians. Wickham further suggests that the difficult term 'interlude', used from the fourteenth century onwards to refer to all sorts of dramatic entertainments,[7] may well derive from the practices of the early professional actors—i.e., the minstrels—who interspersed their variety turns with short dramatic skits.[8] Further corroboration for the suggestion that minstrel troupes did provide the personnel and methods of operation adopted by the later troupes of strolling players derives from the fact that both the minstrel troupes and the troupes of players tended to be small, with the number four mentioned for both classes of entertainer in the records. At Durham Priory we find payment to a group of four *ministrallis domini Principis* performing as early as 1375–6;[9] a group of *iiij ministrallis* of the Duke of Northumberland and *iiij ministrallis domini Northfaolkie* performing at Selby Abbey in 1398;[10] and *iiij^{or} mimis dom. de Arundell* appearing at Winchester College in 1467, when the troupes of players were becoming fairly common. In the year preceding, for example, the *computi* at Winchester College record a payment of 2s to *iiij interludentibus*, and to J. *Meke citharistae* a payment of 4s—both for performing at the feast of Epiphany, probably a Twelfth-Night celebration.

Players of interludes, the *homines ludentes* of the records, in whom we are most interested, begin to appear at the same time as the civic religious drama makes its appearance. At King's Lynn the local chamberlains made a distinction between minstrels and actors in their records as early as 1370. In the town accounts for 1370–1, in an itemized list of payments to troupes of minstrels from the households of such lords as Hereford, Warwick, Oxford, Suffolk, or Lancaster we find the following two entries: *Item de ijs datis menestrallis primo die maij. Item de iijs iiijd datis Ludentibus eodem die.*[11] From then until 1384–5 the clerks merely entered notice of a general item for entertainment, with-

out differentiating between recipients. In that year, however, appears
the following entry: *Et de iijs iiijd solutis quibusdam ludentibus interludium
die Corporis Christi de dono. Et de iijs iiijd solutis ludentibus interludium
Sancti Thome Martiris de dono Maioris.*[12] The next earliest specific
payments of a similar nature that I have been able to discover are the
payments Chambers notes from Rymer's *Foedera* made by the court
of Henry VI at Christmas 1427 to *Jakke Travail et ses compaignons
feisans diverses jeuues et entreludes dedeins le feste de Noell devant notre dit
sire le roi, 4 lib.* as well as to *autres jeweis de Abyndon feisantz autres
entreludes dedeins le dit feste de Noel, 20 sol.*[13] To these payments should be
added such references as the 'laykyng of enterludez' at Christmas in
Sir Gawain and the Green Knight.

From these references it is possible to hazard a guess as to the activities of the early players of interludes. In the first place, they appear to
have chosen times of festival or holiday to make their appearance, in
order to take advantage of the crowds already gathered with money
in their pockets. Given the fact that medieval holidays were generally
on such religious holidays as Christmas, it is not surprising to find the
players at Lynn performing a play on the life of St Thomas, Martyr,
though it is a bit surprising to learn that on one visit their repertory
included a play suitable for Corpus Christi day. On the other hand,
such subjects as are treated in the fragmentary *Interludium de Clerico et
Puella*, apparently a farce, or *Dux Moraud*, a tale of incest and murder,
would be more appropriate for such a thoroughly secular holiday as
May Day.[14] It would seem reasonable to suppose that from their first
appearance the troupes would have a sufficient range of dramatic
material to be able to adjust to the nature of the occasion and the
audience. The remarkably large payment of four pounds to Jakke
Travail and his company suggests that we have here an example of
several plays performed by one company, either in residence, or visiting
for a protracted period of time. The payments of half a mark at King's
Lynn are much more usual amounts for a single performance at this
period, the sums not increasing to even a pound until well into the
sixteenth century.[15]

Except for the two dramatic fragments already alluded to, however,
and the moral play called *The Pride of Life*, also incomplete, we are
pretty much at a loss as to the repertory of these early players. From
their first mention in the records of King's Lynn until the appearance
of *Mankind* approximately one hundred years later, no other plays
survive in English which might have been put on by the small troupes

of players we know existed. On the other hand, a few plays survive which do not fit any of the contexts we have discussed. In this group are such plays as the life of Mary Magdalene dramatized in the Digby manuscript, or the *Play of the Sacrament*. These plays are too elaborate, both scenically and in terms of the cast required, to have been part of the repertory of the early troupes, yet they are unlike any civic performances we can identify. Both show an awareness of the forms of professional drama, as well as the traditions of the cycle plays. To understand the nature of the moral interludes, therefore, we will concentrate on a few fifteenth-century plays which provide the best evidence we have as to the nature of the popular drama of the troupes of strolling players.[16]

What, to begin with, is the best term for these plays? Traditionally such plays have been labelled 'moralities' so consistently that there would seem to be no point in disputing the term. Yet the fact of the matter is that the term morality was not even in general use in the Renaissance period, and not in use at all in the fifteenth century. The plays in question were termed 'interludes', 'moral interludes', or 'moral plays'.[17] Where the civic drama we have been discussing heretofore traditionally presented scenes from biblical history, the 'moral interludes' concern themselves with the life of the individual Christian, and correspond to that great body of sermon literature and moral discourse explicating such articles of faith as the Paternoster or the Credo, as well as instructing the individual sinner in the nature of the path to salvation.[18] Both the Corpus Christi plays and the moral interludes seek to involve the spectator in the life of the play as fully as possible, to provide opportunities for him to identify with the characters of the play so that he may more fully grasp the nature of the doctrinal message purveyed; the 'sentence' as well as the 'solace'. But where the cycle plays do so by individualizing, particularizing the historical characters they present, the moral interludes attempt to universalize their characters as fully as possible, in order to strike a responsive chord in the lives of their audience.

This striving for universality is achieved characteristically through the use of abstractions and generalized names, leading W. R. Mackenzie, in his important study of the subject, to define the morality as 'a play, allegorical in structure, which has for its main object the teaching of some lesson for the guidance of life, and in which the principal characters are personified abstractions or highly universalized types'.[19] The difficulty with such a definition, which has provided the basis for

most subsequent discussions of the plays, is the fact that it has too often
lent support to those who would have it that allegorical drama is a
drama of bloodless abstractions, of stilted characterization, and thus
indeed an inferior mode of drama.[20] Mackenzie himself, however, was
too good a critic to fall into this habit of thought. Recent revivals of the
plays have reminded us, if we were prone to forget, that whenever
'the play was acted, the characters, instead of being dreary types and
abstractions, were at once individualized and humanized; and the
same transformation once took place in the case of every one of the
other Moralities which are now so hastily judged on the basis of the
printed copy.'[21] A possible reason for the persistence of the view that
the moralities, being allegorical, are therefore rather dull may be
the fact that they are usually discussed from a reading acquaintance
rather than from an experience of the plays in production. When one
reads such plays, the row of speakers' names down the left margin of
the page inexorably insists on the allegory through repetition of such
names as *Humanum Genus*, World, Pride, or Good Angel. In production, however, no such effect occurs. Actors, live actors, come and go
on the stage, often dressed in symbolic costumes, but no more so than
were Adam and Eve in the *Jeu d'Adam*. They are infrequently identified by name during the course of the play after their first appearance,
except in ways which are natural to human conversation. Nought,
New Guise, and Nowadays are identified by name twenty-eight times
in the course of *Mankind*, either severally, or as a group. The bulk of
the usage occurs when Titivillus is addressing them directly, and ordering them about. What sticks in one's mind from seeing the play, however, is not the particular names but the character of the three minor
vices given them by their costumes as gallants. Similarly, Mercy's
character as a priest derives primarily from the visual impact of his
costume; Mankind's as a husbandman from his farm labourer's coat.[22]
As a means then of reducing an excessive emphasis on allegory
as essential to the nature of these plays, an emphasis I feel to be
by now unavoidable when the term 'morality' is employed, the
older term 'moral interlude' will be preferred for the rest of our
discussion.

Another reason for de-emphasizing allegory as the primary distinguishing characteristic of moral interludes has recently been indicated
by Robert Potter. According to Potter, allegory is a tool, a means of
expression utilized by the writers of the moral plays, not the basic
identifying characteristic. The primary distinguishing trait of these

plays is their reliance on a particular mode of action for their structure. That action is

a double one: a descent out of innocence into sin, and an ascent out of sin to salvation. The morality play . . . acts out and moralizes three interrelated stages of human existence. The life of humanity is seen to begin in a potential state of innocence but to lapse in the course of experience into an actual state of sin. This state of sin, in turn, is seen to lead by its own contradictions toward the possibility of a state of repentance.[23]

Traditionally the morality plays have been held to derive from the Paternoster plays produced at such cities as York, Beverley or Lincoln in that the seven separate clauses of the Lord's Prayer were held to be specific antidotes for the Seven Deadly Sins. The York play, first mentioned by Wyclif in 1378, is described in a document of 1389 as a play in which 'all manner of vices and sins were held up to scorn, and the virtues held up to praise'. A document of 1399 mentions that one portion of the play was a *ludus Accidie*, or a play of Sloth, one of the Seven Deadly Sins. The Beverley Paternoster play is mentioned in 1469 as containing seven separate pageants, with an additional eighth pageant for *Viciose*.[24] According to this theory, the moral interludes would be one more example of religious dramatic material borrowed by the nascent troupes from the range of civic drama. Corroboration for this line of development is seen in the battle of the Virtues and Vices staged at the centre of *The Castle of Perseverance*, with a venerable tradition supporting such battles in the *Psychomachia* of Prudentius.[25]

The problem with such a purported line of development is that almost none of the other surviving moral interludes, either from the initial period of development in the fifteenth century, or from the period of greatest strength in the early sixteenth century, depend for their basic plot structure on battles between forces of good and evil for the soul of man. On the other hand all, including *The Castle of Perseverance*, follow the pattern that Potter proposes as the basic structure of the plays. The dominant forces seeking the destruction of the central human figure, whether he be single, as in *Mankind* or the *Castle*, or divided, as in *Wisdom* or *Hickscorner*, are the world, the flesh, and the devil. These are the inhabitants of three of the four scaffolds in the *Castle of Perseverance* occupied by the forces of evil, with of all the seven only Avarice—the sin of old age, and the final source of Mankind's fall—occupying a separate scaffold. The other six sins are all subordinate to the three great enemies of mankind. To be sure the Devil himself appears only in *Wisdom* and the *Castle*, but his minions are usually present. The lesson of the moral plays is best summed up by Mercy at the conclusion of *Mankind*:

> Ye hawe thre aduersaryis and he ys mayster of hem all:
> That ys to sey, the Dewell, the World, the Flesch and the Fell.
> The New Gyse, Nowadayis, Nowgth, the World we may hem call;
> And propyrly Titiuillus sygnyfyth the Fend of helle;
>
> The Flesch, that ys the vnclene concupissense of your body.
> These be your thre gostly enmyis, in whom ye hawe put your confidens.
> Thei browt yow to Myscheffe to conclude your temporall glory,
> As yt hath be schewyd before this worcheppyll audiens. . . .
>
> Wherfore, goode sunne, absteyne fro syn euermore after this.
> Ye may both saue and spyll yowr sowle that ys so precyus.
> Libere welle, libere nolle God may not deny iwys.   (ll. 883–94)

As the most recent editor of this text glosses the last line, '"Freely to will, freely not to will" [God may not deny certainty]'.[26] These plays are studies in the choices man makes, the recurrent opportunity to fall, in which man is no inert battlefield over which the forces of good and evil march but a being with free will created by God whose chances to choose the right road to salvation end with the coming of death. *Everyman* is part of this pattern, if it is recognized that the fall has taken place before the play begins, and that the motif of the summoning of Death is only a fragment of the larger pattern. To see how the pattern works in practice let us turn to two representative plays of this group, *Mundus et Infans* or *The World and the Child*, and *Mankind*.

Neither of these plays is traditionally taken as an example of the norm, as representing the traditions of the plays of the professional troupes. *Mundus et Infans* was not included in J. Q. Adams' influential anthology of *Pre-Shakespearean Dramas*, and was thus until recently only available in a Tudor Facsimile Text published in 1907.[27] *Mankind* was included, but in a bowdlerized version. The former play has thus generally been ignored, and the latter until recently attacked as dreadful stuff, poorly written, and in bad taste besides.[28] Yet there are good reasons to consider them typical examples of the staple fare offered during the fifteenth century by the touring professional companies. Both require only small casts, and utilize doubling patterns effectively. Both have been shown to work well in modern theatrical settings. *Mankind* is particularly interesting in its use of vulgarity and slapstick

---

spyll destroy

comedy to achieve its desired effect—a good collection from the audience. Finally, both exemplify the pattern of innocence, fall (or falls), and eventual rebirth through repentance, that typifies the *genre* of the moral interlude.

. Of the two, *Mundus et Infans*, though later, is the better play with which to begin, as its structure is more apparent.[29] The play opens with the figure of the World enthroned, possibly in a booth similar to that depicted on Wynkyn de Worde's title page. However, it is more probable that the stage which the writer had in mind was the simple booth stage, raised on trestles or barrels, with a curtain at the rear for the quick costume changes required, with a throne the single property on an otherwise bare stage.[30] The World, a 'ruler of realms', speaks from his throne, then, in the costume of a regal figure, using the bombastic alliterative language of all medieval stage rulers. The World quickly indicates the nature of his power. 'He that cometh not when I do him call, / I shall him smite with poverty' (ll. 15–16). Thus when the Child appears on stage, emphasizing the precarious state into which man is born—'Poor and naked as ye may see' (l. 45), defenceless, in constant fear of death—the World's power is translated into terms which make the Child's first fall thoroughly predictable. Mankind, at his birth, needs food and clothing to preserve his existence. His own flesh betrays him into the power of the World while he is still an innocent, before the age at which he can be aware of sin. Where in *The Castle of Perseverance* Mankind makes a deliberate choice of food and clothing at the urging of the Bad Angel, and is subsequently invested in the clothing of a knight as his reward, the writer of *Mundus et Infans* places the event prior to the beginning of the age of reason.[31] The Child's first fall is less a matter of choice than of necessity.

Two costume changes, and two alterations in language, carry the Child to Manhood while the World watches benevolently from his throne.[32] While there is no particular sin indicated during this period in the life of the Child, the language given him as Wanton (age seven to fourteen) and as Love-Lust-Liking (age fourteen to twenty-one) characterizes him as a rather selfish, self-centred person. Wanton is effectively limned as a spoiled child by his catalogue of favourite games. Love-Lust-Liking is notable for his excessive sensuality—'Might I find a fode that were fair and free / To lie in hell till doomsday for love I would not let' (ll. 137–8). However, when the Child reaches

---

fode companion *let* leave off

Manhood, and fully possesses reason, World takes command of his vassal. In return for the power of a knight that is granted to him, Manhood must become the embodiment of a proud, overbearing, extortionate member of the nobility.

> Bear thee prest in every game
> And wait well that thou suffer no shame
> Neither for land nor for rent. (ll. 160-2)

The Seven Deadly Sins, subservient here (as in the *Castle*) to the World, are mentioned to Manhood as 'kings' to whom he owes allegiance. Upon his formal agreement to follow World's injunctions, Manhood is invested as a knight, with the appropriate regalia, and his fall is complete. The symbolic transfer of worldly power that accompanies that fall is represented once World has vacated the stage by Manhood's first ranting, alliterative soliloquy, as well as ascent to World's now vacant throne.

Each stage in Manhood's development is concluded by a soliloquy delivered by the figure of Manhood. As Professor Bevington has indicated, soliloquies are not functional in the plays written for civic drama, be they for place-and-scaffold or pageant wagon.[33] Cain may address the audience with the contempt of despair in the Wakefield *Mactatio Abel*, the kings and tyrants or their precursors may beat a path through the audience with speeches addressed to them as they pass, or figures such as *Contemplacio* in the N-Town cycle may comment directly on the action that is taking place: but, generally speaking, soliloquies in which the central character reflects on his state are virtually non-existent. For the civic drama is a theatre primarily of action. Action is important to the professional drama as well, as we shall see in *Mankind*. At the same time, periodic costume changes required by the doubling patterns of plays written for professional companies absolutely require that the stage be held by one or at the most two figures, generally at the conclusion of a unit of the action of the play.

It is to the credit of the playwright constructing the doubling pattern in *Mundus et Infans* that each soliloquy contributes to our understanding of the hero's internal development rather than simply providing a weak cover. In the first soliloquy, as we have seen, Manhood assumes worldly power. In his second, Manhood reflects on the moral instruction that Conscience has just given him. Where the writer of the *Castle of Perseverance* objectifies the internal debate that follows such instruction in the allegorical siege of the Castle, demonstrating his adherence to the older methods of representing internal debate worked out in such non-dramatic allegories as *The Romance of the Rose*,[34] the writer of *Mundus et Infans* provides his central character with a vacillating speech, in which he wavers between adherence to the advice of Conscience and his old allegiance to the World. In such a state, Folly can appropriately enter. Manhood's third soliloquy, the shortest of the three, presents his formal decision to follow the suggestions of Folly, and signals his second fall. Conscience, covering what must be an extensive alteration in Manhood's costume as he changes to the third and last stage of man's life, Age, comments on the nature of Folly, specifically drawing the connection between Folly and the Devil, but he does so in the form of direct address we are familiar with in such preaching figures as *Contemplacio*:

> Lo, sirs, a great example you may see,
> The frailness of mankind
> How oft he falleth in folly
> Through temptation of the Fiend,
> For when the Fiend and the flesh be at one assent
> Then Conscience is clean outcast.   (ll. 716–21)

Within each unit of the play framed by these soliloquies the successive stages of the pattern of man's fall and recovery from sin are handled with the economy and precision possible when one is writing within a highly developed tradition—the tradition of penitential literature.[35] The costume changes of the actor representing the forces acting upon the central character correspond to alternative phases in the road toward salvation or damnation, phases so constant that they can still form the sequence of events in C. S. Lewis' *Screwtape Letters*. Having assumed earthly power, Manhood's Conscience is aroused, but this is Conscience conceived more as a general knowledge of right and wrong than as a sense of personal sin. Just as Manhood has a specific identity as a knight, so too does Conscience, who enters in the garb of a friar. Once he is accosted by Manhood, he sets immediately about his task of instruction, educating Manhood as to his true state. The lesson that characterizes this unit of the play is cast in the form of a catechism, whose purpose is to explicate the nature of the seven 'kings', and to teach Manhood his proper function. Six of the seven are shown to displease God, but Manhood is allowed, even forced, to maintain his allegiance to the seventh, Covetous. However, Conscience then develops Manhood's knowledge further by drawing on the well-worn conventional medieval dichotomy between the two forms of love, *caritas* and *cupiditas*—love and cupidity, or covetousness—to demonstrate that what Manhood must properly covet is eternal life. Interpreting the Ten Commandments in terms of Christ's injunction to 'Love thy neighbour as thyself', the basic text for an understanding of *caritas*, Conscience then leads Manhood on to knowledge of his function as a knight. Instead of using his power for extortion,

> Ye must, Manhood, with all your might
> Maintain Holy Church's right,
> For this longeth to a knight
> Plainly in every place. (ll. 443–6)

When Manhood objects, fearing the loss of his 'game and glee', a concern that is to have consequences in the subsequent unit of the play, Conscience assures him that 'mirth in measure is good for thee' (l. 449). Conscience also allows appropriate apparel, and play in due proportion, but warns against 'folly and shame' (l. 488). On this warning, he exits.

Through this knowledge Manhood has been brought to a general understanding of sin, and a knowledge of the path to eternal life. But knowledge of sin does not necessarily lead to the will to avoid sin. As already indicated, Mankind does indeed reflect on the knowledge he has gained. But the conclusion he reaches, despite the fact that he admits the truth of what Conscience has taught him, is finally to choose the World, quite consciously, for the same reason he chose it in the first instance—'For both in church and in cheaping / And in other places being / The World findeth me all thing / And doth me great service' (ll. 512–15). Once again man is betrayed by the needs of the flesh. However, this time Manhood gives an additional reason for choosing the way of the World. 'Now mirth is best' he proclaims. On these words, Folly, the agent of the Devil, enters, ushering in the next phase of the life of man.

What we are watching is not a psychomachia, a struggle for the soul of the protagonist conducted by the rival armies of good and evil, but plays which seek as effectively as possible to universalize the patterns of moral choice in man's life. The forces bent on mankind's destruction rely on their powers of persuasion, on trickery, and on inherent weaknesses within the human constitution itself to bring man to the

cheaping market

wrong choice. But that choice is always his. From the figure of Man-kind in the *Castle of Perseverance* to Marlowe's Dr Faustus each character in the *genre* of the moral interlude understood that the choice of the heavenly path was always possible, and could be made up until the dying breath.[36] Thus the task for the forces of evil once Man has almost inevitably fallen to the temptation of the world is to keep him constant in his determination to follow the broad road to Hell. This task normally falls to the Devil or his substitutes, the Vice figures.[37]

Virtually every characteristic of the Vice figures is already present in the characterization of Folly, who dominates the scene of Manhood's second fall. He enters on the standard note of vulgarity common to all medieval stage devils, responding to Manhood's request that he show proper courtesy with the remark 'What, I do but claw mine arse sir, by your leave' (l. 526). Otherwise there is no immediate identifying mark of the Devil about him. Folly must be wearing a form of fool's clothing, and arrives carrying a pan of some sort, as well as something with which to conduct the mock combat with Manhood that ensues. Professor Spivack believes that the slapstick humour which is the normal means of expression for these minions of the Devil represents 'the unregenerate instincts of playwright and audience'. The 'grave theme' of these plays, the perpetual fall of men, 'was accepted and respected, but in order to hold the allegiance of mere flesh and blood it required its countertheme, and the whole morality drama is marked by its large concession to farcical stage business and verbal humour'.[38] Considering the generally high tone of *Mundus et Infans*, one hardly conceives of its author as 'unregenerate'. The term when applied to the author of such a play as *Mundus et Infans* in fact smacks of the same problem to which we addressed ourselves in our study of 'realism' in the cycle drama. And the same answer holds true for the moral inter-ludes that we found to be true of the rude vulgarity of the detractors in *The Trial of Joseph and Mary*. The farce and broad humour, when used properly, demonstrate indeed the irreverence of the satanic crew and provide a vehicle through which they can express their contempt for their victims. But as in the case of Raise Slander and Backbiter, this irreverence is not something which the audience is asked to share. If anything, it should act to distance the vice from the sympathies of the audience. Yet because the moral interludes were presented to a paying audience, which was indeed unregenerate in many cases, and certainly for the most part unlearned, the temptation to overdo the part of the

Vice, to provide more 'solace' than 'sentence' was always present. To
this problem we will return in assessing the balance of farce and sentence in *Mankind*.

What is important here is to note that the conventional qualities
which are part of the Vice's characterization are all present in the
character of Folly. He is, as one would expect, contemptuous of
Conscience: 'A cuckoo for Conscience, he is but a daw / He can not
else but preach' (ll. 623–4) is his response when Manhood realizes that
Conscience has warned him against Folly. He is equally contemptuous
of his victim. Once Manhood has agreed to Folly's suggestion that he
be hired as Manhood's servant, and has proposed that they drink to the
bargain, 'For that is curtesy', Folly gives a servant's properly deferential response—'Marry master, ye shall have in haste' (ll. 645–6). He
then turns to the audience to tell them

> Ah ha, sirs, let the cat wink,
> For all ye wot not what I think.
> I shall draw him such a draft of drink
> That Conscience he shall away cast.   (ll. 647–50)[39]

Because the audience is meant to be under no illusion as to Folly's
nature, his speech is seen to be consistently ironic. For example, as
Manhood is preparing to embark on his career of lechery and carousing
in the stews of London, he worries that someone will recognize him.
Folly reassures him, 'An thou will go thither with me / For knowledge
have thou no care' (ll. 665–6). Schell and Shuchter gloss this as meaning
that no one will recognize Manhood where he is going so long as
Folly is with him, and in one sense this is correct. He will be so trans-
formed that this will be the case. On another level the line means what
it says; Manhood will indeed have no care for the knowledge of salvation that Conscience gave him if he goes to the stews. When Folly has
outlined the life of drinking and wenching that is conventional to the
fallen state Manhood asks hopefully 'What sayest thou, Folly? Is this
the best?' to which Folly answers 'Sir, all this is manhood, well thou
knowest' (ll. 674–5). Finally, the vice figures are as thoroughly didactic
as those on the side of the angels, educating the audience through direct
address as to their true nature. So Folly, as he exits, tells the audience
precisely how he operates. Having given the clothing of Shame to
Manhood as a disguise, fulfilling his promise to transform him
beyond recognition (a promise unfulfilled as far as Conscience is

concerned, as the subsequent short scene will show), Folly then explains his function:

> Come after, Shame, I thee pray,
> And Conscience Clear ye cast away.
> Lo sirs, this Folly teacheth aye,
> For where Conscience cometh with his cunning
> Yet Folly full featly shall make him blind;
> Folly before and Shame behind,
> Lo, sirs, thus fareth the world alway. (ll. 691–7)

It only remains for the actor playing Folly to exit, throw a friar's robe over his fool's garb, and return to make the equation between Folly and the Fiend explicit, for the moral lesson of this portion of the play to be hammered home.

At the conclusion of Conscience's speech, the stage clears completely, ending the second age of man. Because this is a drama of repentance in which the protagonist is saved, the final portion of the play consists of moral instruction by Perseverance, who enters first and identifies himself (he is probably costumed as a priest or a monk, certainly a religious of some sort) as Conscience's born brother. He is followed by Manhood, now identified both by his appearance and formally in his speech as Age, who gives a reprise of the preceding action, and then summarizes the life in sin that he has led, bringing himself to the inevitable state of despair and the contemplation of suicide. Perseverance, however, brings Age from despair to a state of repentance, reminding him that the way to heaven requires that

> ... with great contrition ye must begin,
> And take you to abstinence,
> For though a man had do alone
> The deadly sins everychone,
> An he with contrition make his moan
> To Christ our heaven king,
> God is also glad of him
> As of the creature that never did sin. (ll. 856–63)

The remainder of the play consists of instruction in the means to persevere in grace; that is, the proper use of the five 'bodily wits' and the five powers of the soul as well as belief in the twelve articles of faith and knowledge of the sacraments and the Ten Commandments. Perseverance in all these will lead to salvation. And on this note the play ends.

The pattern described here persists throughout the life of the moral interlude. It is the pattern of the *Castle of Perseverance*; it is found in such late hybrid moralities as *Cambises*; it is the pattern that Marlowe follows in *Dr Faustus* and that underlies *Othello*, though there less overtly. Not all the pattern need be present in a single play. *Everyman* begins with the life in sin, omitting the period of man's youth, achieving its remarkable effects by concentrating only on the process of repentance itself in the face of death. But we must never forget that the use to which the pattern is put is dictated primarily by the author's perception of what will appeal to the audience-for-a-day to whom the troupes of professional players addressed their plays. From the extraordinary compression of the cast in *Mundus et Infans* one suspects that it was written for special circumstances. More likely to represent the average play offered for acting by the troupes in the fifteenth century is the moral interlude *Mankind*.

That the play was written for a professional troupe is clear from the moment in the play when the action stops for a collection to be taken. Titivillus, the comic devil, has just farted offstage, and can be expected at any moment. The three minor vices, representing the forces of the World, at this point turn to the audience asking for their 'red royals' (gold coins worth ten shillings) or, if none are forthcoming, groats or pence. When the collection has taken place, Titivillus appears, and the play resumes. The collection begins with 'the goodeman of this house', which suggests, as does a later request that the hostler bring a football, that the play was intended for an inn yard. The audience posited is clearly mixed; Mercy opens the play with an address to 'ye souerens that sytt and ye brothern that stonde ryght uppe'.[40] Mercy's opening warning to the audience to 'Dyverte not yowrsylffe in tyme of temtacyon' suggests further that the audience originally intended is best conceived of as drinking in an inn or tavern when the players arrive. Yet the demands of the play are so minimal—no scenery is required, and no props that could not be easily carried into the acting area—that it really is best to think of the play as infinitely adaptable. Given these marks of professionalism it is reasonable to suppose that the leading actor in the company played both the part of the priest Mercy and of Titivillus, leaving the cast requirement at six.

The pattern of the play's central action is close to that we have established for *Mundus et Infans*. Mankind appears at the beginning of the second age of man, already in a fallen state as a result of the rebellion of the flesh.

> My name ys Mankynde. I haue my composycyon
> Of a body and of a soull, of condycyon contrarye.
> Betwyx them tweyn ys a grett dyvisyon;
> He that shulde be subjecte, now he hath the victory. (ll. 194–7)

As a means of rectifying this condition he goes to Mercy for spiritual instruction. Mercy advises him to use moderation in the fight between the body and the soul. Appropriately for an audience holding tankards of ale in their hands, Mercy advises Mankind to 'Dystempure not yowr brayn wyth goode ale nor wyth wyn. / Mesure ys tresure. Y forbyde yow not the vse. / Mesure yowrself euer; be ware of excesse' (ll. 236–8). Mankind then sets to work digging in his pasture. When one considers the pervasive references to man's work in agricultural terms in the parables of the New Testament or the virtue attached to such figures as Piers Plowman in late medieval satire, one recognizes that Mankind is not digging because the audience contains many farmers. Mankind is able to resist the first attack by Nought, New Guise, and Nowadays, forces of the World, all characterized by their idleness, and in fact drives them from the stage with his spade.

But as Manhood found with Folly, victory in physical combat with the forces of evil provides no long-term security. Titivillus, whom Mercy had already identified as 'worst of them all', engineers Mankind's fall by an assault on the weakness of the flesh. The digging grows hard (a board is put in the earth to make it so), darnel is spread in the corn that Mankind has planted, and Mankind despairs. Unlike Nought, New Guise, and Nowadays, Titivillus is invisible, and works through suggestion rather than in the open direct manner of the forces of the World. His primary ally within Mankind's nature is, as one would expect, the flesh, who betrays Mankind through the sin of Sloth. From a reluctance to continue his labour, Mankind progresses to praying in the field because it is too much trouble to go to church. That praying is interrupted by the need to relieve himself, which leads in turn to the loss of his Paternoster beads (Titivillus actually filches them, but one can equally well conceive of them as simply being lost). From the loss of his beads Mankind progresses to a complete state of Sloth, falling asleep on stage. While he sleeps, Titivillus completes his work by sending a dream in which Mankind believes he sees Mercy stealing a horse and a cow, and being hanged for it. Waking from this dream, Mankind chooses consciously to take the same path taken by Manhood, 'I wyll hast me to the ale-house / Ande speke wyth

New Gyse, Nowadays and Nought / And geett me a lemman wyth a smattrynge face' (ll. 609–11). The life in sin is represented by a scene in which Mankind swears to follow the life of thuggery his new-found fellows pursue, during which his suitable and serviceable long coat is cut down to a ridiculous short one supposedly in the very latest fashion. The conclusion of the life in sin is reached with the return of Mercy. Mankind despairs, and the three wastrels try to oblige him by assisting him to commit suicide. They bungle it, however; in fact, New Guise almost hangs himself while demonstrating how it is done, and they exit, leaving Mankind to be brought back to a state of grace through Mercy's recognition of his true state of repentance.

This action, however, occupies only about half the play. What gives the play the bulk of its energy are the broad farce and the antics of the three representatives of the World and their companion Mischief. Not only has this farcical element been found by some hard to swallow but what seems worse, it appears to undercut with extraordinary effectiveness the homiletic message of Mercy. For example, Mercy opens the play with a direct injunction to the audience to 'Pryke not yowr felycytes in thyngys transytorye' (l. 30), but instead to remember the Day of Judgment and to order their lives accordingly. When he reaches the point in his sermon when it becomes appropriate to re-mind the audience that on that Last Day, 'The corn shall be sauyde, the chaffe shall be brente', Mischief suddenly bounces onstage to point out that that particular oratorical chestnut is really too much. All the audience would have heard it too often to count, and so he proceeds to suggest that the dichotomy does not work, since horses eat straw, and men burn straw for heat. Thus straw, or chaff, is not useless, not a proper symbol for that which will be thrown out on the Last Day. Later, when the three wastrels have replaced Mischief as Mercy's tormentors, New Guise calls attention to Mercy's excessively aureate vocabulary. After Mercy has rhymed 'denomynacyon' and 'com-munycacyon', New Guise cries out 'Ey, ey! yowr body ys full of Englysch Laten' (l. 124).

Because we ourselves in reading the play find Mercy's Latinate vocabulary pompous and rather ludicrous (and we may note that Mankind adopts the same language in his conversations with him), we assume that the audience would have sided with New Guise. Because the 'corn-chaff' chestnut had been used to death, we assume

---

smattrynge ? pretty   *Pryke* fasten

that Mercy's doctrine is equally trite. And because Nought, New Guise, and Nowadays enter dancing, opting for mirth, and singing funny scatological songs of the type we associate with an evening of beery gaiety after a good dinner, we assume, perhaps too quickly, that they attract the sympathies of the audience, undercutting the morality. However a second reading of the play, or attendance at a modern production, quickly dispels this impression. Though amusing at first, the vices quickly become insufferable. Their banter, their unwillingness to allow anything to be taken seriously, their 'idle language', as Mercy calls it, rapidly palls as it does in real life. Their humour becomes funny only to themselves. Mercy's doctrinal speeches are indeed heavy going, and the three wastrels fasten precisely on those qualities which the audience might find absurd themselves. But when Mercy warns Mankind that they will soon be upon him, we do not look forward to Mankind's confrontation, eagerly awaiting his downfall as we must if we side with the fallen angels. No, Mankind's insistence that he must get on with his work acts to preserve our sympathy; and as the mockers dance about him, driving him to break out in exasperation, 'Haue ye non other man to moke, but euer me?', we find our sympathies so totally on the side of the protagonist that his attack on them with his spade comes as a welcome relief.

The matter is more serious than simply idle language. If we had any lingering doubts as to the nature of World's agents during the first section of the play, they should be completely dispelled once Titivillus has joined the company. He first asks each of the minor vices if they have any money about them. All have just completed their collection, so it is obvious to the audience that when Nought is joined by the others in proclaiming that his purse is as clean as a bird's arse, he and the rest are lying through their teeth. At this point Titivillus turns to the audience to aver a second time that 'Her ys an abyll felyschyppe to tryse' the good horses of the audience 'out of yowr gatys', (l. 491). He then proceeds to send the three off to rob the countryside of Cambridgeshire (i.e., the area in which the audience lives). Titivillus next sets to work managing the fall of Mankind. At the moment when Mankind announces that he is off to the tavern to wine and wench with the World, New Guise bursts in with a broken halter around his neck, having escaped near-hanging. Nowadays arrives with the plate he has stolen from a neighbouring church, which shall pay for the ale, bread

---

tryse snatch

and wine that Mankind intends to share, and Mischief arrives with
some food and drink he has stolen from the jail, still carrying his
fetters, having broken out of jail by killing the jailer. These are no gay
lads, no jolly fellows, but examples of the scum found in every town
and city both then and now, who support their idle life by a career
of armed robbery. The local allusions are meant to bring home to the
audience that losses they have recently suffered—I suspect that the
names chosen refer to men known to have been robbed in the neigh-
bourhoods mentioned—were caused by men very similar to the
gallants onstage. It is hard to argue for much audience identification
with such rogues! Thus when Mankind, clearly oblivious to what the
three wastrels are telling each other, begs their pardon and asks to
join their company because he has dreamt that Mercy is dead, Nowadays correctly guesses that only Titivillus could have brought off this
'conversion'. Mankind's subsequent degradation, symbolized primarily in the truncation of his garment to a ridiculous, and probably
indecent, length is a fitting consequence of his decision to join such a
crew.

Recognition that the forces of the World and the Devil as embodied
in the vice figures of the moral interludes are apt embodiments of sin
should never blind us to the very real comedy they create onstage.
Here, for example, is the sequence following Mankind's discovery
that Mercy is alive, and returning:

> *Myscheff.*   How, Mankynde! Cumm and speke wyth Mercy, he is
>   here fast by.
> *Mankynde.*   A roppe, a rope, a rope! I am not worthy.
> *Myscheff.*   Anon, anon, anon! I haue yt redy,
>   Wyth a tre also that I haue gett.
> Holde the tre, Nowadays, Nought! Take hede and be wyse!
> *Neu Gyse.*   Lo, Mankynde! do as I do; this ys thi new gyse.
>   Gyff the roppe just to thy neke; this ys myn avyse.
> *Myscheff.*   Help thisylff, Nought! Lo, Mercy ys here!
> He skaryth ws wyth a bales; we may no lengere tary.
> *Neu Gyse.*   Qweke, qweke, qweke! Alass, my thrott! I beshrew
>   yow, mary!
> A, Mercy, Crystys coppyde curse go wyth yow, and Sent Dauy!
> Alasse, my wesant! Ye were sumwhat to nere.   *Exiant* (ll. 799–810)

The frantic preparations for Mankind's suicide as Mercy approaches,

---

bales scourge   *wesant* throat

when Nought and Nowadays struggle to hold up a piece of a tree, undoubtedly working at cross-purposes, with New Guise's demonstration of the proper way to place the rope suddenly interrupted by the frantic scattering of the vices as Mercy enters sternly carrying a scourge, leaving him momentarily strangling—all this is broad farce, and up-roariously funny. In 1969 a group of students took a production of the play on tour through the pubs of Cambridge during May Week. Generally the patrons of the pubs did not know that the play was to be put on; thus the audience was not composed of scholarly students of the drama with prudish preconceptions. What they saw and responded to was a very funny play. At the same time, Mercy's dialogues with Mankind were attended to, and apparently appreciated. One can hardly imagine such an audience attending in the same way, in the same surroundings, to a play with any less farce or comedy. If this is to be unregenerate, then indeed audiences have always been and always will be such. It is to the credit of the author of *Mankind* that he knew how to mingle 'sentence' and 'solace' in effective measures to create a thoroughly successful professional play.

Native English dramatic comedy of the late medieval period consistently relies on rough slapstick and scatological language for most of its effects. Cain beats Garcio about his stage, Lucifer falls from Heaven crying 'For fere of fyre a fart I crake', other devils and vices run on and off stage with burning squibs in their costumes, Folly and Manhood beat each other around the stage in a slapstick parody of a duel. All of these elements persist throughout the sixteenth century. Ambidexter enters in *Cambises* 'with an old capcase on his head, an olde paile about his hips for harnes, a scummer and a potlid by his side, and a rake on his shoulder' to engage subsequently in a knockabout slapstick fight with Huf, Ruf, and Snuf. Covetous, the Vice in *Enough is as Good as a Feast*, throws himself into a rage at his assistants Precipitation and Temerity and a fight breaks out. The comedy can be achieved through spectacular theatrical effects as well. In the *Play of the Sacrament* the activities of the Jews in attempting to destroy the Host are all handled as farce. Their leader, Jonathas, picks up the Host at one point, and it sticks to his hand. The stage direction reads 'Her he renneth wood, with the Ost in hys hond.'[41] The rest nail the hand with the Host in it to a post with three nails, and then try to pull the arm off the Host. Instead, the arm comes off. Following the intrusion of the

---

wood mad

comic doctor and his assistant from the folk plays, the Jews beat them off the stage, heat up a cauldron, and seek to boil the Host to pieces. Instead, the cauldron bursts, and streams blood. Fergus the Jew loses his arm when he attacks the bier of the Virgin in the Assumption play at York, and in the N-Town version he sticks to the bier. With this tradition to work with, it is not surprising to find the Jew of Malta exiting into a burning cauldron.

If this in fact is the dominant tradition of English stage comedy, as it appears to be, then we can understand why John Heywood's delightful farces modelled on French sources, such as *Johan Johan* or *The Pardoner and the Friar*, struck no roots in English soil, and why no other adaptations of the large body of surviving medieval French farces and *sotties* are found in the drama of England in the fifteenth and sixteenth centuries. Reading through the jestbooks from the same period one is struck by the same phenomenon. The Fools of Gotham beat each other on the bridge at Nottingham in a foolish argument over non-existent sheep both in the *Merry Tales of the Mad Men of Gotham* and *The First Shepherds' Play* of the Wakefield cycle; but very few jests relish the pranks of students and lecherous priests as they find their ways to the beds of the willing wives of aged husbands. Both love and comedy in a cold climate take different turns than they do in the warmer countries of Europe; the Three Stooges and the comics of the pantomimes are part of a venerable native tradition stretching back beyond the moral interludes to the mimes, *joculatores* and *homines ludentes* about whose repertoires we know so little. And as we come to know the moral interludes of the sixteenth century better through successive revivals it becomes clear that the morality of these plays can exist in a far more comfortable union with their elements of broad farce than up to now we have been willing to admit.

6

OF HISTORY AND TIME

Assessing the relative vitality of the older forms of dramatic activity and the new forms that were developing in the early sixteenth century is an extraordinarily difficult task. Earlier historians of the drama, interested primarily in the drama of the Renaissance, tended to assume that civic religious drama was largely senescent by the turn of the century, and searched through the interludes and classical schoolboy plays for the origins of the Elizabethan theatrical traditions. As we have seen, the civic religious drama of medieval England survived with considerable vigour until the early years of Elizabeth's reign, to be systematically put down for political reasons rather than dying of its own weight.[1] Civic records for cities such as Coventry, York or Chester demonstrate that this dramatic tradition was essentially conservative, preserving those forms and traditions worked out in the fifteenth century that we have already analysed. Similarly the theatrical conventions of the street pageants prepared for royal entries continue in an unbroken process of very gradual evolution from their fourteenth-century beginnings. The men who were experimenting with new dramatic forms of expression belonged to a world in which these older forms were still part of their normal experience.

John Rastell is a case in point. By most standards that have been applied in the past he stands as an embodiment of the new Renaissance spirit, concerned to find new forms of literary expression, which characterized the reigns of Henry VII and Henry VIII. He was imbued with the sense of national identity that supposedly marks the members of newly emerging nation states. This patriotism is expressed most clearly in his interlude on *The Nature of the Four Elements*, where he affirms his belief in England's destiny to become a great colonial power on the model of Spain and Portugal following the discoveries on England's behalf made by John Cabot.[2] He himself undertook to make a voyage to the 'new found land', but was abandoned by his mariners in Ireland when he refused to sanction their desire to substitute piracy for discovery as the object of the voyage.[3] Rastell set up one of the early printing presses, whose invention is so often associated with the creation of the new reading public of the Renaissance, and he, and later his son, printed the plays of Medwall, John Heywood, possibly Skelton's *Magnificence*, as well as Rastell's own plays. As F. P. Wilson puts it, 'Fragmentary as is our knowledge of early sixteenth-century drama, without the Rastells it would have dwindled to a point.[4]' These plays are usually taken to mark the beginnings of humanist drama in England; the break with the traditions of the past. Certainly *The Four Elements*, with its emphasis on instruction in the nature of this world rather than in the way to the next represents an attempt to adapt an older dramatic form to the new purposes of humanism.

Yet we must be cautious in following these leads. The caveat of one of the most learned students of the drama of this period, F. P. Wilson, is worth repeating:

Humanism is a word to avoid in any consideration of early English drama, for if it means the ability to write humanistic Latin, our dramatists were much better occupied in making their own language more expressive; and if it means the recovery of Greek, they never recovered Greek, and even after readers of English came to know Sidney's *Apology* with its Italian interpretation of Aristotle's *Poetics*, all but a few dramatists ignored every precept they were advised to follow.[5]

Rastell uses the medieval interlude form for his play on the elements; Medwall's *Fulgens and Lucrece* dramatizes an Italian source, to be sure, but does so in the form of a debate, a form already venerable when employed in *The Owl and the Nightingale*. Rastell prints the first English jest-book, the *Hundred Mery Tales*, but the collection itself is nothing more than a culling of the humorous tales from the collections of *exempla* used by the medieval preachers.[6] And Rastell, who grew up watching the royal entries and Corpus Christi plays we have already described in the city of Coventry, himself designed a street pageant erected at the little conduit by Paul's Gate for the entry of Charles V and the King to St Paul's in 1522, a pageant which undoubtedly borrowed its staging from a play representing the Assumption of the Virgin.[7]

And so it goes. Old forms of drama are used as a vehicle for new ideas, continue to have a life of their own, often a life possessing considerably more vitality than the new classical imitations that do begin to appear in university and court circles as the century progresses. *Ralph Roister Doister*, which appears in nearly every anthology of sixteenth-century drama as exemplifying the new winds of classicism, is in fact a windy, rather dull play, possessing none of the energy which *Gammer Gurton's Needle* derives from its sturdy reliance on the traditional English comic staples of farce and broad language. One factor undoubtedly curtailing the spread of humanism much beyond the small circle associated with More was the onset of the religious controversies of the mid-century. Rastell died in prison for his over-zealous support of church reform; he was, in his own words, 'now by long imprisonment brought to extreme misery, forsaken of his kinsmen, destitute of his friends, comfortless and succourless'.[8] John Heywood, whose uncharacteristic farces we have already noted, saved himself from execution for treason after involving himself in a plot against Cranmer by publicly recanting, but ended his life in exile after Elizabeth ascended to the throne. More's tragic inability to preserve his urbanity and his life as well as his independence while serving Henry VIII has been the subject of more than one recent dramatic production. Until the Elizabethan settlement was secure none of the new directions pioneered by men like Rastell could develop into modes of expression capable of stirring audiences throughout England.

Not only the dramatic forms and conventions of the type we have been examining, but also medieval habits of thought, the basic ideas of what constituted reality and the nature of the universe, continued to influence the drama of the sixteenth century. A singular example of how a key medieval conception, of great influence in forming the structure of the civic Corpus Christi cycle drama, survived to influence the later drama of the sixteenth century will serve to illustrate how pervasive were medieval habits of thought in the drama which succeeded the drama of England's Middle Ages on the public stage. The conception I wish to examine is the medieval notion of history.

Writing of the historical patterns of thought in Shakespeare's history plays, O. B. Hardison recently proposed that

After all the qualifications based on order of composition, departures from the larger pattern, and ambiguities of Tudor political theory have been accepted,

the plays remain something more than a haphazard collection, and their unity
is that of the medieval religious cycles.[9]

Yet Hardison's proposal that the conception of history contained in
the cycle plays of the Middle Ages could be a major influence on the
later histories flies in the face of the received doctrines as to the sources
and influences acting on the *genre* of the history play which supposedly
makes its first appearance in the mid-sixteenth century. E. M. W.
Tillyard admitted that the moralities had exerted 'a pervasive influence
on all Shakespeare's history plays', but felt that even they had 'not
had a great deal to do with the ideas about history' on which the later
history plays were built.[10] What the actual influence of the moralities
was he did not spell out. It is probable he had in mind some such
influence as that proposed subsequently by Irving Ribner. Ribner,
who specifically rejected the cycle plays as influencing the later histories because of their purportedly disorganized episodic structure,[11]
proposed that 'The morality play structure was a perfect vehicle for
executing the true historical function, for the morality was didactic
and symbolic, designed to communicate idea rather than fact, built
upon a plot formula in which every event was related to the others
so as to create a meaningful whole'.[12] According to both Tillyard and
Lily B. Campbell,[13] the historical ideas, that is, the historiography,
which would provide the basis for the pattern Dr Hardison perceives,
stemmed not from medieval drama but from such sixteenth-century
works as the *Mirror for Magistrates* by way of *Gorboduc* and the later
so-called 'chronicle plays'.[14] Neither Campbell nor Tillyard even
mentions the cycle drama.

Certainly the conventions developed by the writers of interludes as
well as the historical orientation of such writers as Hall and Holinshed
had an influence on both the form and content of the *genre* of the Elizabethan history play. An equally formative influence, however, the
cyclic view of history, derived in the first instance from conceptions
of time developed in the early Christian period and later embodied in
the English medieval mystery cycles. Campbell has claimed that 'It
is on the assumption that history repeats itself that political mirrors of
history can be utilized to explain the present'.[15] But this assumption
is not one of the historical concepts peculiar to the Renaissance. No-
where can medieval notions of the cycles of history be seen so well as in
the civic plays which portray the history of the world from its creation
until its end. Following the formal and explicit banning of plays on
religious subjects by a succession of monarchs in the sixteenth century,

however, the dramatists of the later sixteenth century were forced to develop an alternative body of historical narrative material for dramatic presentation, while still employing the dramatic conventions developed to present the earlier cycles of sacred history. When these dramatists had at their disposal a body of historical material as well-known to their audiences as sacred history had been known to their fore-fathers, then and only then could they create an analogous historical drama.[16]

To understand the correspondences between medieval and Elizabethan dramatic formulations of history we must review once again the conventions governing the form and content of the earlier plays. Both Sepet's older theory of the origins of cycle form as a 'budding out' of the Prophet plays and the more recent theory of Chambers, Young, and, following them, Craig, that cycles consist of an assemblage of translated Latin liturgical plays plucked out of different liturgical feasts, have been modified in the light of V. A. Kolve's analysis of the historical conceptions governing cyclic form. As we have seen, the purpose behind the institution of the feast of Corpus Christi in the first instance was 'to *celebrate* the Corpus Christi sacrament, to explain its necessity and power, and to show how that power will be made manifest at the end of the world'.[17] The manifestations of that power which give the cycles their underlying structure are the Three Advents of God into human history, listed in a medieval sermon as follows:

> Frendes, for a processe ye shull vndirstond that I fynde
> in holy writt iij commynges of oure Lord; the first was
> qwen that he com to make man; the secound was qwen he com
> to bie man; and the iij shall be qwen he shall com to deme man.[18]

These divine interventions into human history provide the conventional opening of the cycles, the plays presenting the life of Christ from the Nativity to the Resurrection and Ascension and the traditional ending in the Last Judgment. Here is the working of Divine Providence in its clearest form.

In addition to the anticipated scenes from the life of Christ, the cycles include other material, however. It is this other material which gives the Corpus Christi drama its cyclic quality. A group of plays dealing with scenes from the Old Testament regularly occur. Two principles appear to be at work in the process by which these scenes were selected. One such principle is that of the *exemplum*, where an historical event is simply adduced to point a moral. To this we will return later. Of more importance is the method of interpreting Old Testament figures in terms of the New, known as figural interpretation. Erich Auerbach, in his essay entitled simply 'Figura', traced the development of the term *figura* down through the classical period to Quintilian, during which it developed meanings still current in discussions of poetic tropes and figures of speech. With Tertullian, however, another meaning develops, a meaning which derives its use from the practice of 'phenomenal prophecy'. A *figura* 'is something real and historical which announces something else which is also real and historical'. According to Auerbach,

> figural interpretation establishes a connection between two events or persons, the first of which signifies not only itself but also the second, while the second encompasses or fulfils the first. The two poles of the figure are separate in time, but both, being real events or figures, are within time, within the stream of historical life. Only the understanding of the two persons or events is a spiritual act, but this spiritual act deals with concrete events whether past, present, or future, and not with concepts or abstractions.[19]

Figural interpretation differs from allegory, where the effort is to transform the historical events of the Old Testament into purely spiritual significations. An historical event treated as a *figura* can be considered separately from the immediate context in which it occurred, but it is never anything but a real event.[20] Thus in the 'Prima Pastorum' of the Wakefield Pageants in the *Towneley Cycle*, the foolish shepherds having become wise through revelation supply the spiritual links between events in the Old Testament and the Nativity.

> 1 *Pastor.* Of (the child) spake more: Sybyll, as I weyn,
> And Nabugodhonosor from oure faythe alyene;
> In the fornace where thay wore, thre childer, sene,
> The fourt stode before, Godys son lyke to bene.

> 2 *Pastor.* That fygure
> Was gyffen by reualacyon
> That God wold haue a son;
> This is a good lesson
> Vs to consydure.[21]

A. C. Cawley in his notes to this and related passages, indicates the traditional nature of such figural interpretation.[22]

    Other traditional figural interpretations of the incidents from the

---

Nabugodhonosor Nebuchadnezzar

Old Testament are regularly included in the cycles.[23] For example, the story of Cain and Abel is dramatized not just because it was the first murder, but also more importantly because the protagonists are *figurae*—Abel of Christ, in his capacity as the first martyr, and Cain of the envious Jews. The poet of the *Meditations of the Life and Passion of Christ* contrasted Abel's blood as crying for revenge with Christ's crying for mercy, a development of Hebrews xii, 24.[24] This is the difference between the Old Law and the New. Or, the *figura* of Abraham and Isaac can be used to indicate not only that Isaac is a *figura* or type of Christ, but that Abraham's willingness to sacrifice his son makes it possible for God to sacrifice his in fact. The Expositor of the Chester version is the only one to underline the figural significance of this play, but his interpretation is clear:

> This deed you se done in this place,
> In example of Ihesu done yt was,
> that for to wyn mankinde grace
> was sacrificed on the rode.

> By Abraham I may vnderstand
> the father of heaven that can fand
> with his sonnes blood to break that band
> the Devil had brought vs too.

> By Isaac vnderstand I may
> Jhesu that was obedyent aye,
> his fathers will to worke alway,
> his death to vnderfonge.[25]

Not every Old Testament figure, however, appears in the cycles. The fiery furnace of Nebuchadnezzar may be cited by one of the prophetic shepherds, but it does not even appear in *The Play of Daniel*.[26] The principle of selection governing the choice of Old Testament figures to be included in the medieval English cycle plays derives from the fundamental postulates of medieval historiography, particularly the division of historical time into epochs or periods. R. G. Collingwood, in *The Idea of History*, proposed that the characteristics of Christian historiography which determined the medieval viewpoint were as follows:

i) It will be a *universal* history, or history of the world, going back to the origin of man . . .

---

and endeavour

This is so because in the sight of God, all men are of equal importance.

(ii) It will ascribe events not to the wisdom of their human agents but to the workings of *Providence* preordaining their course . . .

(iii) It will set itself to detect an intelligible pattern in (the) general course of events, and in particular it will attach a central importance in this pattern to the historical life of Christ, which is clearly one of the chief preordained features of the pattern. It will make its narrative crystallize itself round that event, and treat earlier events as leading up to or preparing for it, and subsequent events as developing its consequences . . .

This is the thinking which lies behind the technique of figural analysis we have already noted.

(iv) Having divided the past into two, it will then naturally tend to subdivide it again: and thus to distinguish other events, not so important as the birth of Christ but important in their way, which make everything after them different in quality from what went before. Thus history is divided into epochs or *periods*, each with peculiar characteristics of its own, and each marked off from the one before it by an event which in the technical language of this kind of historiography is called epoch-making.[27]

The specific periods or epochs chosen to be dramatized in the cycles were the seven ages of the world culminating in the sabbath of eternal rest with which St Augustine concludes *The City of God*.[28] St Augustine defines these ages as follows:

The first age, as it were the first day, is from Adam unto the flood, and the second from thence unto Abraham, not by equality of times, but by number of generations. For they are found to have the number ten. From hence now, as Matthew the evangelist doth conclude, three ages do follow even unto the coming of Christ, every one of which is expressed by fourteen generations. From Abraham unto David is one, from thence even unto the transmigration into Babylon is another, the third from thence unto the incarnate nativity of Christ. So all of them are made five. Now this age is the sixth, to be measured by no number, because of that which is spoken. 'It is not for you to know the seasons, which the Father has placed in His own power.' After this age God shall rest as on the seventh day, when God shall make that same seventh day which we shall be, to rest in Himself . . . But this seventh shall be our sabbath, whose end shall not be the evening, but the Lord's day, as the eighth eternal day.[29]

No epoch-making figure of the stature of Adam, Noah, Abraham, and David appeared in the age of the Transmigration into Babylon, Augustine's fifth age. Jechonias, the father associated with this age on the basis of Matthew i, 11, is ultimately replaced by Moses and the Exodus on the basis of Bede's five-part division, 'based on the five hours in which the labourers in the vineyard were hired'. Bede's five periods were those of the Creation, Noah, Abraham, Moses, and Christ; considering the prevalence of the Old Law–New Law dichotomy in medieval thought it is not surprising that Exodus replaces the Transmigration in many medieval divisions of history.[30] Whichever pattern is followed, the sixth age remains the same—contemporary history; in this pattern it can be treated as are all other epochs.

The conception of the seven ages of time, and the treatment of the Patriarchs as *figurae* explain the relations of the parts to the whole of the cycles. Reference to the present time of the audience, the time of the sixth age, could also be made through another application of history. For historical events not only relate to other events as announcements of God's providential plan, they can also serve as self-contained lessons for the present. *Any* event from the past can also become an *exemplum* for the present, providing an illustration of cause and effect with moral consequences. Cain in the Towneley Cycle may be murdering the first martyr, himself a type of Christ, but the character of Cain which the Wakefield Master develops is that of the medieval farmer who beats his servant and cheats on his tithes. God's refusal of Cain's sacrifice becomes a commentary on God's judgment of similar actions in the time present of the audience. Or there is the long list of imaginary characters whose names are in the book of Den, the Summoner, in the N-Town *Trial of Joseph and Mary*, all contemporary medieval English names, such as 'Symme Smalfeyth and kate kelle / and bertylmew the bochere'. The apparently anachronistic habit medieval dramatists have of developing their characters as medieval stereotypes derives not so much from a lack of historical imagination as from an historical view in which events in the present mirror events in the past. For the cyclic view of history implied by the theory of the seven ages leads to the belief shared by both medieval and Renaissance writers that in its patterns 'history repeats itself'. Thus not only sacred history, dramatized so to speak in 'medieval dress', but all forms of history hold precedents for the present, in so far as the patterns found there recur in the field of human action. It is but a small step from the Fall of Adam to the Fall of Princes. For the medieval dramatist, as for Ranulph Higden or Raphael Holinshed, the study of history had the double benefit of teaching God's purposes manifested in the epochs of history and inculcating moral lessons in the sphere of politics and ethics.

Both the figural and the exemplary applications of historical material can be seen at work in the drama of mid-sixteenth-century England. First, as regards the figural view of history, it is not difficult to see how the representation of one real historical event as announcing another later real historical event, originally applied to interpretations of the Old Law in terms of the New, could be extended to any two historical events within the cycles of time. Thus the dramatist of *Godly Queen Hester* employs the figure of Esther to illuminate the situation of Katharine of Aragon, just as a pageant writer had used the figure of King Ahasuerus to comment on Richard II nearly 150 years earlier.[31] A more instructive example of the figural use of history to interpret secular rather than sacred events, is Bale's *King John*. In the Interpretour's speech which divides the two acts Bale makes the following identifications:

> Thys noble kyng Iohan, as a faythfull Moyses,
> Withstode proude Pharao for hys poore Israel,
> Myndynge to brynge it owt of the lande of Darkenesse.
> But the Egyptyanes ded agaynst hym so rebell
> That hys poore people ded styll in the desart dwell,
> Tyll that duke Iosue, whych was our late Kynge Henrye,
> Clerely brought vs in to the lande of mylke and honye.
> As a stronge Dauid at the voyce of verytie,
> Great Golye, the pope, he strake downe with hys slynge,
> Restorynge agayne to a Christen lybertie
> Hys lande and people, lyke a most vyctoryouse kynge,
> To hir first bewtye intendynge the churche to brynge,
> From ceremonyes dead, to the lyuynge wurde of the Lorde.[32]

This speech, written either under Edward VI or for the presentation of the play under Elizabeth, explicitly equates John and Henry VIII with illustrious Biblical predecessors. Each gains his identity from the type to which he corresponds.

But Bale's identifications go much further than this. John himself is a *figura* for Henry VIII; both are antagonists of Antichrist! The fulfilment of the figure only comes about fully with the second monarch.[33] Sedition promises that as a result of the tricks of the troop of vices, 'We iiij by owr craftes Kyng Iohn wyll so subdwe / That for iij C. yers all Englond shall yt rewe' ([I], ll. 775–6). When at the beginning of Act II (ll. 121–33) Clergye outlines how the interdiction will operate to bring

Iosue Joshua

John round, he is also indicating the forces that Henry VIII has over-
come. Bale's handling of the vice roles—Sedition as Stephen Langton,
Usurped Power as the Pope, or Private Wealth as Pandulphus—is an
extension of Bale's figural handling of the major character. The type
is recurrent, the individual is important only as a manifestation of the
type at a particular moment in history. As a recent student of Bale's
work has put it:

It is evident that Bale thinks of the evil characters as being first and foremost
perennial representatives of evil; their occasional appearance as historical
characters in a specific situation is used by way of *exemplum* to lend credence to
their existence on a 'higher' plane.[34]

Bale, as is necessary in figural interpretation, insists on the historicity
of the events he depicts, even if they are presented in the abstract forms
of the morality rather than in the specific historical surroundings of
the cycle drama. Nobility opines early in the play that 'kyng Iohn ys
lyke to rewe yt sore / Whan ye wryte his tyme, for vexcyng of the
clergye' ([I], ll. 588–9). As the play draws to its close, following John's
poisoning, Verity assures the audience directly that 'Kynge Iohan was a
man both valeaunt and godlye. / What though Polydorus reporteth
hym very yll / At the suggestions of the malicyouse clergye? / Thynke
yow a Romane with the Romanes can not lye?' ([II], ll. 2194–7).
Instead Leland is invoked to put things right. And as history the sad
tale is also an *exemplum*, a cautionary tale for others beside the king.
After Nobility has been rebuked by Imperial Majesty (Henry VIII himself?) for hearkening to Sedition, Nobility recalls,

> I consydre now that God hath for Sedicyon
> Sent ponnyshmentes great. Examples we have in Brute,
> In Catilyne, in Cassius, and fayer Absolon,
> Whome of their purpose God alwayes destytute,
> And terryble plages on them ded execute
> For their rebellyon.   ([II], ll. 2604–9)

These same 'examples' reappeared a number of times in the drama that
was to follow, teaching not only Nobility to avoid the blandishments
of Sedition. But of the two uses of history, the cyclic rather than the
exemplary dominates Bale's thinking.

Few interludes from the end of Henry VIII's reign or those of
Edward VI and Philip and Mary survive to indicate how typical was
Bale's adaptation of older methods of interpreting history for his own
polemic purposes. Clearly, whatever its ostensible subject, polemic

drama was sufficiently widespread during the period to call for such acts as the *Act for the Advancement of true Religion and for the Abolishment of the Contrary* in 1543, which forbade 'interpretacions of scripture, contrary to the doctryne set forth or to be set forth by the kynges maiestie'.[35] That such interpretation could be somewhat more subtle than Bale's is suggested by the play of *Jacob and Esau*, properly praised by F. P. Wilson as a well-made play along classical lines,[36] but at the same time undoubtedly a studied Calvinist attempt to 'justify the seizure of power, and to insist that the seizure is reluctantly undertaken'.[37] Professor Bevington correctly observes that the playwright 'is less concerned with informing his audience about Old Testament history than with seeing the original story as a type of current history'.[38] *Jacob and Esau*, though licensed in 1557–8, must belong, by its temper, to the period of Edward VI. I suspect that the biblical interlude, *The Tower of Babylon*, produced at court for Christmas 1548, was likely to have involved a cautionary example of some sort as well. In any event, the series of acts catalogued by Chambers,[39] and reviewed recently by Wickham,[40] culminating in the act of 1559 which formed the basis for the Elizabethan control of the stage, all indicate that drama from this period had been consistently polemic. But it should be stressed that it was the specific applications of history, not the methods of interpretation, that had become offensive.

Much of the polemic drama was produced in the capital. In the provinces the older cycle plays were only polemic in that their production tended to be identified with Catholic sympathies. Hence the attempts to preserve the cycles by expunging offensive material, such as the Marian plays Martin Stevens believes were deleted from the Towneley Cycle.[41] But the end of dramatized biblical history was nearing. In the Act of 16 May 1559 Elizabeth charged the officers in the towns and cities

That they permyt (no plays) to be played wherein either matters of religion or of the governaunce of the estate of the common weale shalbe handled or treated, beyng no meete matters to be wrytten or treated vpon, but by menne of auctoritie, learning and wisedome, nor to be handled before any audience but of graue and discreete persons: All which partes of this proclamation, her maiestie chargeth to be inuiolably kepte.[42]

To be sure passing a law and enforcing it are two different matters.[43] Father Gardiner quotes a report solicited by the Privy Council in 1564 which indicated that 'of a total of 851 justices, only 431 were favourable

to the government policy in matters of religion'.[44] Yet slowly but
surely the Privy Council overcame such obstacles; the melancholy
story of the suppression of the cycles as detailed by Father Gardiner is
now thoroughly familiar.

What is of interest to students of early English drama is that where
known replacements for the cycles are found they are still historical.
At Coventry an Oxford student named Smith was engaged to write
a play on the *Destruction of Jerusalem*. A possible source is a book cited
by Lily B. Campbell as an example of Reformation history. Joseph
ben Gorion's history of the Jewish people was translated in 1558 by
'Peter Morwyng (or Morwen) of Magdalen College in Oxford' and
ran through nine editions from then until 1615. In his preface Morwyng
cites the value of this history as follows:

The history of the Jews could teach Christians useful lessons. . . . As when thou
seest the Jews here afflicted with divers kinds of misery, because they fell from
God: then maist thou be admonished hereby to see the better thine owne
waies, least the like calamities light upon thee. . . . Thou shalt read here of
terrible and horrible eventes of sedicion and rebellion . . . in so muche that
nothing hastened their destruction so greatlye as their own doggishness and
intestine hatred. Be thou warned therefore by their harmes, and take hede
that thou maist avoid the like.[45]

Coventry's play was commissioned for 1584, and was played again in
1591. At Shrewsbury, Thomas Ashton, master of the free school, in
1566 produced a play on Julian the Apostate. At Lincoln the St Anne's
day cycle was discontinued after 1555. Later, in 1564, the Common
Council determined that a 'standing play of some story of the Bible
shall be played two days this summertime'.[46] The play decided on in
that year was 'the story of olde tobye', i.e., the new biblical history
play was based on the apocryphal book of *Tobit*.[47] This play was produced until 1567. A surviving list of properties strongly suggests that
'the standing play of old Tobey' was a stationary production utilizing
many of the properties surviving from the earlier St Anne's day play,
if not the Corpus Christi cycle which had become defunct earlier. In
each case the history chosen appears to have been designed to fulfil
traditional expectations in the audience without violating the injunction
against treating matters of religion (that is, disputed doctrine) on the
stage.

The plays at Coventry, Shrewsbury, or Lincoln, like the play of
Samson put on at the Red Lion Inn in 1567, or Thomas Garter's *The
Most Virtuous and Godly Susanna*, also of the 1560s, indicate that the

first attempts to find alternative historical material were conditioned
by the audience's expectations inherited from the past. Granted that
the sacred history of the cycles was no longer safe from state control,
might not biblical or early Christian history not directly associated with
the Christian religion prove a safer substitute? In point of fact, it does
not seem to have done so, any more than did *Gorboduc*. For to the
Elizabethans, as to the medieval audience, all history is instructive,
either in a figural sense, where one event announces the nature of one
to follow, or in an exemplary sense, as a cautionary tale. Too many
generations of glossators and commentators had worked over the
corpus of biblical material for any of it to be innocent of applications to
contemporary events, since it is the interpreter who makes history a
matter for polemics. Thomas Norton and Thomas Sackville were
just as guilty of violating the statute of 1559 as were writers of new
biblical plays, for if *Gorboduc* does nothing else it deals with 'the
governaunce of the estate of the common weale'. During the dramatic
doldrums of the 1570s Harbage's *Annals* lists numerous titles drawn
from classical history, demonstrating that Horestes and Cambises' vein
proved for a while to be the safest to mine. Classical history and romance
provided the bulk of the dramatic material produced until the end of
the 1580s. By then the Elizabethan settlement was relatively secure;
what had once been controversial could now be tolerated. English and
biblical history alike return to the stage with *The Famous Victories of
Henry V* in 1586; and *Job*, and Peele's *The Love of King David and Queen
Bethsabe*, in 1587. But Peele's play was the end of a line. In the words of
the play's most recent editor, *David and Bethsabe* stands alone in the
Elizabethan period as an extant English play based completely on the
Bible.[48] English, rather than sacred history, became the staple dramatic
fare, but still a history conceived of in cyclic terms where both king
and commoner could learn of God's purpose for man. In dramatizing
that history the Elizabethan playwrights had at their disposal the
dramatic conventions developed to present cyclic patterns, namely the
figural and exemplary conventions of the medieval mystery cycles.
These conventions, rather than an Aristotelian plot, are what give
the Elizabethan history plays their unity, and provided a means of easy
communication between artist and audience.

Our interest in the drama of medieval England does not derive from
its relative impact on the drama of Elizabeth's reign. The word 'pre-
Shakespearean' is best dropped in describing the plays with which we

have been concerned, for it throws the focus of attention forward in time, away from the fifteenth and early sixteenth centuries when one of England's great periods of dramatic activity took place. Yet so many fine studies of the drama of this early period have been undertaken by scholars first drawn to it through their love of Shakespeare, and their interest in the origins of the theatre in which he worked, that this bias is by now almost ingrained in studies of medieval English drama. My attempt here has been rather to approach that drama from the point of view of a medievalist, to propose a variety of approaches to that drama which treat it as worthy of study in its own right. The survival of any part of that drama into the succeeding age is only an incidental reason for our interest in its workings, just as our interest in the survival of theatrical traditions from the Caroline stage is only incidental to our appreciation of the Restoration stage. What we must never forget as we read the small corpus of plays which survive from this early period is that the traditions and habits of thought which give them their life were well-established by the mid-fifteenth century, and that drama had a continuing life thereafter of over one hundred years. The same cannot be said of the drama from any other period in English literature. It thus behoves us as students of the past to search out as effectively as we can the sources from which that drama derived its strength, to under-stand its traditions and conventions, as well as the ideas on which it is based. That search cannot fail to be rewarding.

NOTES

Preface

1. George R. Coffman's article 'A Plea for the Study of the *Corpus Christi Plays as Drama*', *Studies in Philology* **26** (1929), 411–24, was in fact the first to urge that the plays be taken more seriously, but his plea went unheeded.

Chapter 1. Locating the plays in space and time

1. *The Macro Plays*, Ed. Mark Eccles, EETS **262** (London 1969), xxi.

2. For the plan, see Eccles ed., frontis.: for a translation of the text, see p. 1. The plan with the text translated is often reproduced, as in J. Q. Adams' anthology, *Pre-Shakespearean Dramas* (Cambridge, Mass., 1924), 264.

3. See, for example, Richard Hosley, 'Three Kinds of Outdoor Theatre Before Shakespeare', *Theatre Survey* **12** (1971), 1–14.

4. For a discussion of this position, see Natalie Crohn Schmitt, 'Was There a Medieval Theatre in the Round?', *Theatre Notebook* **23** (1969), 1–13, esp. 12–13, and **24** (1970), 14–21. Mrs Schmitt proposes that the ditch is part of the playing area, and cites as evidence the 'watyr of grace' referred to in line 2329. As further evidence one might note that during the siege of the castle, Sloth attempts to make a 'dyke drye' (l. 2352) with a spade. Merle Fifield, in 'The Arena Theatres in Vienna Codices 2535 and 2536', *Comparative Drama* **2** (1968–9), 259–82, also questions Southern's thesis.

5. For the reference to Selby Abbey, see M. C. Bradbrook, *The Rise of the Common Player* (London 1964), 25; for King's Lynn, see E. K. Chambers, *The Mediaeval Stage* (London 1903, hereafter cited as *MS*) II, 374.

6. See Chapter 5 for Glynne Wickham's discussion of this point in *Early English Stages, 1300–1600* I, *1300–1576* (London 1963), 266 ff.

7. David Bevington, in *From Mankind to Marlowe* (Cambridge, Mass., 1962), 49, believes that 'little doubling was possible and was probably not considered necessary', proposing rather that the thirty-six roles, including the bann-criers, 'May have been divided between professional strollers and an assortment of amateurs drafted from each locality'. But as Eccles (*Castle*, xxii) reasonably

demurs, 'only one character, Penance, speaks fewer than forty lines'. Local talent
seems hardly up to the task of acting the necessary parts.

8. *Ludus Coventriae*, Ed. K. S. Block, EETS ES **120** (London 1922), 16, ll. 525–
528. Because the cycle in question has no localizing references it is often called by
the name of a former owner, Robert Hegge. An erroneous ascription to the city
of Coventry by a seventeenth-century cataloguer has produced the alternative
title, *Ludus Coventriae*. Part of the Coventry cycle survives, and bears no relation
to this manuscript. Under the circumstances the best solution to the problem of
nomenclature is to refer to this cycle as the N-Town cycle, from the passage at
the end of the banns.

9. Giles Dawson, *Records of Plays and Players in Kent, 1450–1642*, Malone
Society, *Collections* VII (Oxford 1965), 119–27.

10. The only reference I have found to such a phenomenon is the payment of
6s 8d, a crown, at New Romney in 1463–4 for a play of the interlude of the
Passion of our Lord from 'Agneti fforde'. See Dawson, *Plays and Players*, 120.

11. Wickham, *Early English Stages* I, 168–74.

12. ibid., 173. Wickham's diagram appears on this page.

13. See M. James Young's consideration of this problem in 'The York Pageant
Wagon', *Speech Monographs* **34** (1967), 1–20 esp. 7.

14. M. James Young cites a 1415 ordinance which states that 'the play "shall
be played before the doors and houses of those who are willing to pay most
richly and well to the chamber" and does not mention that these people must live
on the widest streets' (ibid., 9).

15. What the result would be if the wagon were wheeled around to a position
at right-angles to the street, as my wife proposed on reading this passage, is
worth speculation. One effect would be to double the number of rentable
windows! However, I have seen no discussion of this idea as yet.

16. *English Literature at the Close of the Middle Ages* (London 1945, hereafter
cited as *Eng. Lit. at the Close*), 27.

17. ibid., 30.

18. *The Drama of Medieval England* (E. Lansing, Mich., 1961), 135.

19. The effect of asking the wrong questions, of using the wrong yardsticks,
can be seen most clearly in Hardin Craig's *English Religious Drama of the Middle
Ages* (London 1955, hereafter cited as *ERD*) of which the following paragraph,
taken from his introduction, provides a signal example:

> When one considers the origin of the mystery plays within the medieval
> church, an origin without thought of dramatic or histrionic effect, and when
> one considers also how these plays passed into the hands of very simple medieval
> people—authors, players, managers, and all—one can see that their technique
> was inevitably naive and firmly conventional. Their distances were symbolic
> distances, and their time symbolic time.... The drama of the medieval
> people was anachronistic because it was symbolic and not realistic and because,
> like most Elizabethans also, its portrayers had not in the modern meaning an
> historical sense. This drama had no theory and aimed consciously at no dramatic
> effects, and, when it succeeded, its success came from the import of its message
> or from the moving quality of some particular story it had to tell (p. 9).

Drama whose 'successes' are the result of mindless simplicity is hardly likely to score often. Because the plays about which he was writing were not like those of Ibsen, Craig could find no critical vocabulary to assess their worth, despite his obvious erudition.

20. W. W. Greg, 'Textual and Bibliographical Problems of the English Miracle Cycles', *The Library*, 3rd ser., 5 (1914), 389; K. S. Block, *Ludus Coventriae*, xv, xxiii–xxiv.

21. *York Plays* (Oxford 1885; repr. New York 1963), xviii–xxviii. Harbage's *Annals of English Drama, 975–1700* (London 1964), by now a standard modern reference work, dates the manuscript even later, *c.* 1475.

22. *Wakefield Pageants* (Manchester 1958), xxi. In Harbage's *Annals* the text as a whole is dated '*c.* 1390–1410 (?) (originated)', adding that 'the work of the Wakefield Master may have begun *c.* 1435 and extended to *c.* 1450' (p. 8).

23. Greg, 'Textual Problems', 187.

24. Salter, *Medieval Drama in Chester* (Toronto 1955), 49. While on this point, it should also be observed that the manuscript of the surviving Cornish cycle, an altogether separate affair, is dated in Harbage's *Annals* '1400–1500'!

25. Craig, *ERD*, 133.

26. Chambers, *Eng. Lit. at the Close*, 21.

27. Greg, 'Textual Problems', 290–1.

28. *English Drama from Early Times to the Elizabethans* (London 1950), 71. The frontis. to Rossiter's study, a detail from a Grünewald painting of the Crucifixion, showing the grotesque faces of the torturers, sums up what Rossiter found most attractive in the plays. We will return to this point in Chapter 4.

29. ibid., 66–7.

30. F. M. Salter, *Medieval Drama in Chester*, 40–2. See also Wickham, *Early English Stages* I, 133–42.

31. Salter, op. cit., 41–2.

32. Wickham (*Early English Stages* I, 125) ties the development of the cycle plays to the practice of civic ridings for ceremonial occasions.

> From the outset [the Festival of Corpus Christi] took the form of a ceremonial procession, the detail of which was left to local enterprise and initiative to supply. An example of how to manage it was already to hand in the pageantry of civic ridings. In these the guilds had carried symbols of their trade for many years and by 1377 were initiating short mimetic performances on fixed stages. Since records of 'Corpus Christi Plays' only start after 1377 it is reasonable to suppose that developments of these plays paralleled the development of the civic ridings in both date and kind.

One further date is traditionally offered as proof for the purported sequence of events in the fourteenth century. This is an expenditure in 1350 of half a mark by William de Lenne and his wife, on joining the guild of Corpus Christi, for a *ludus filiorum Israelis*, probably a play on the Slaughter of the Innocents (Chambers, *MS* II, 109 and 344). This is virtually the sole evidence for cycle plays in England before the Beverly date of 1377! Yet the Cambridge reference is in all probability not to a cycle play at all. Salter queried Chambers' assumption that it was (*MS* II, 130) on two counts: '(1) Was it not a Latin play? (2) Was it not produced by a religious, rather than a craft guild?' (*Medieval Drama in Chester*, 119). Inasmuch as religious guilds were as likely to sponsor cycle drama as the craft guilds, this last is not a serious objection. More important is the fact that half a mark is a normal fee for a single play in account books until the sixteenth century, though the fees do creep up to a crown and a mark as the fifteenth century progresses. See Giles Dawson, *Plays and Players in Kent*, xviii–xix.

33. What use was made of the older chronology is indicated by the following quotation from Craig, *ERD*:

> In approaching the study of the English mystery plays chronology is also important. The matter is one of great difficulty, since records are scarce, and the work of scholars in the field is full of misapprehensions. Throughout the period of 250 years—from the beginning of the fourteenth until slightly beyond the middle of the sixteenth century—religious plays were undergoing in various places and at various times continual amplification and revision. As the plays were revised and rewritten, they grew regularly farther from their Latin sources and also, let us say, farther from their simple vernacular beginnings. At the opening of the fourteenth century, and perhaps for a large part of that century, most of the mystery plays must have been scarcely more than amplified translations or paraphrases of Latin originals. They probably followed Scripture or liturgy closely, and they were written in old and simple metres and stanzas. In the long preservation of these poetic forms we find a useful key to the chronological development of the mystery plays. (p. 159)

It is high time we concentrated not on what might have been, but on what has survived.

34. For further discussion of this subject, see Kenneth Cameron and Stanley J. Kahrl, 'The N-Town Plays at Lincoln', *Theatre Notebook* **20** (1965–6), 61–9, and 'Staging the N-Town Cycle', *Theatre Notebook* **21** (1967), 122–38, 152–65; also my *Records of Plays and Players in Lincolnshire, 1300–1585*, Malone Society *Collections* VIII (London 1974).

35. E. J. Dobson, in 'The Etymology and Meaning of *Boy*', *Medium Aevum* **9** (1940), 146, states that the *Ludus Coventriae* is a Norfolk text. Norman Davis, in a personal communication, has corroborated Dobson's conclusions on the basis of his work on the Paston letters.

36. Eccles, *Macro Plays*, xi.

37. In addition there is a marginal note that the manuscript belonged to 'Hyngham, a monk'. Eccles (ibid., xxviii) located a Thomas Hingham at Bury St Edmunds in the fifteenth century, a Thomas Hengham at Norwich around the middle of that century, and a Richard Hengham or Hyngham as abbot at Bury from 1474 to 1479.

38. *Non-Cycle Plays and Fragments*, EETS SS1 (1970), lviii–lxii, lxx, lxxxv.

39. ibid., cxi.

40. 'The Late Medieval Plays of MS Digby 133: Scribes, Dates, and Early History', *Research Opportunities in Renaissance Drama* X (1967) 163.

Chapter 2. The major theatrical traditions

1. Chambers, *MS* II, 62–3.

2. See O. B. Hardison, Jr's discussion of this point, *Christian Rite and Christian Drama* (Baltimore 1965), 253–83.

3. The usual title for the first play is the *Mystère d'Adam*, translating the Latin *Ordo Representacionis Ade*, as in the edition by Paul Aebischer (Geneva 1964). More easily accessible, however, is the translation by Richard Axton and John Stevens in *Medieval French Plays* (Oxford 1971). I shall therefore use their titles, and quote from their translation. Cross-references to Aebischer's edition are noted as well.

4. Axton and Stevens, *French Plays*, 7.

5. Wickham, *Early English Stages* I, 48.

6. Axton and Stevens, *French Plays*, 24.

7. The Latin wording—*ut amenissemus locus videratur*—recalls the *topos* of the *locus amoenus*. See E. R. Curtius, *European Literature and the Latin Middle Ages*, Tr. Willard R. Trask (New York 1953), 195–200.

8. Axton and Stevens, *French Plays*, 36; Aebischer, *Ordo*, 70.

9. Axton and Stevens, *French Plays*, 13; Aebischer, *Ordo*, 35.

10. Axton and Stevens, *French Plays*, 13; Aebischer, *Ordo*, 35.

11. Axton and Stevens, *French Plays*, 33; Aebischer, *Ordo*, 65. In the fifteenth-century English morality, *Mankind*, to which we will return in Chapter 5, the hero, Mankind, is brought to his fall by the agent of the Devil, Titivillus, in exactly the same way. See *Mankind* in the *Macro Plays*, Ed. Eccles, 171, ll. 537–48.

12. Axton and Stevens, *French Plays*, 18; Aebischer, *Ordo*, 44.

13. O. B. Hardison, commenting on this point, remarks that 'Frequent instructions to the players . . . indicate an advanced acting technique'. (*Christian Rite and Christian Drama*, 282–3).

14. See *Masks, Mimes and Miracles*, (1931; repr. New York 1963), 196–205, for many of the known early illustrations of medieval plays.

15. Axton and Stevens, *French Plays*, 49.

16. ibid., 48.

17. See Nicoll, *Masks*, 16.

18. *Beverley Town Documents*, Ed. A. F. Leach, Selden Society (London 1900), 45 (the page of translation is given the same page number as the Latin text).

19. ibid., 33–4. The Latin text reads: *ludos et pagentes paratos amodo qualibet die in festo Corporis Christi, modo et forma secundum antiquam consuetudinem ville Beverlaci, ad ludendum in honore Corporis Christi.*

20. ibid., 34.

21. ibid., 35. Leach used 'stage' instead of 'pageant' to translate the final use of *pagenda* in this entry.

22. ibid., 109.

23. ibid., 99.

24. However, Chambers, *MS II*, 161 actually prefers to read this entry as describing a procession of dumbshows, and not plays at all. One sees how difficult it is to discuss the matter under these circumstances.

25. Grace Frank, *Medieval French Drama* (London 1954), 165.

26. (New Haven 1892). Others have subscribed to this idea as well. See W. Creizenach, *Geschichte des neueren Dramas* I (Halle 1893), 169 ff.; L. Petit de Jul-leville, *Histoire du théâtre en France, Les Mystères*, (Paris 1880), 186–216; M. Lyle Spencer, *Corpus Christi Pageants in England* (New York 1911), 61 ff.

27. *MS* II, 161.

28. Hardin Craig (*ERD*, 134, 137) presents the reasons why *tableaux vivants*

were ignored in reconstructions of the early history of the pageant wagons as follows:

> The plays could not have come from the figures in the procession, because the plays were in existence long before the procession was instituted . . . the particular set of subjects treated in the Corpus Christi plays are there, not because they were chosen to suit the idea of Corpus Christi, or because they were dramatically attractive in themselves, but because they were the liturgical themes and events handed down for centuries and thus ready to be combined into cycles on the occasion of the establishment of the feast of Corpus Christi (with its procession) in the early fourteenth century.

29. V. A. Kolve, *The Play Called Corpus Christi* (Stanford 1966), 48.

30. Wickham, *Early English Stages* I, 51–111.

31. ibid., 51.

32. An excellent reproduction of Pieter Brueghel's depiction of such a stage can be found in Bamber Gascoigne's *World Theatre* (London 1968), 104. For a discussion of such stages, see Gascoigne, 113–14; also Hosley, 'Three Kinds of Outdoor Theatre', 24–5.

33. Wickham, *Early English Stages* I, 54.

34. *Two Coventry Corpus Christi Plays*, EETS ES **87** (London 1957), Appendix III, 109–18, and frontis. See also Craig's discussion of the stations, introd., xiii–xiv.

35. M. D. Anderson, *Drama and Imagery in English Medieval Churches* (Cambridge 1963), 37.

36. Craig, *Coventry Plays*, 110.

37. ibid., xiii.

38. Wickham, *Early English Stages* I, 55.

39. Salter, *Medieval Drama in Chester*, 54–7.

40. See L. M. Clopper, 'The Structure of the Chester Cycle: Text, Theme and Theatre' (dissertation, Ohio State Univ. 1969) for a discussion of the accuracy of Rogers' account.

41. Salter, *Medieval Drama in Chester*, 56.

42. Craig, *Coventry Plays*, 84.

43. Salter, *Medieval Drama in Chester*, 68–70, having collected irrefutable indications of the use of roofs on the wagons, is particularly hard on Rogers in the matter of a roof. For good reproductions of the wagons at Louvain and Brussels, as well as a sympathetic discussion of Rogers' account, and a good drawing by Richard Southern of what a wagon stage may have looked like, see Hosley, op. cit., 14–24.

44. The six wheels are still a problem. Alan Nelson has studied this feature of the description, even to the point of visiting a surviving six-wheeled gun carriage in the Victoria and Albert Museum. See his article 'Six-wheeled Carts: An Underview', *Technology and Culture* **13** (1972), 391–416 for a discussion of the difficulties encountered in steering such a vehicle. Hosley, op. cit., 21, notes that 'We need only suppose that the rear axle of a six-wheeled wagon was mounted on a pivot and connected by a pair of cross-chains with the front axle, in such a way as to require the rear wheels to turn equally but opposely with the front wheels'. Since the structures at Louvain and Brussels have four wheels, let us leave this as an unresolved puzzle.

45. Williams, *Drama of Medieval England*, 97–8. M. James Young, 'The York Pageant Wagon', 13, used a maximum stage size of ten feet by twenty feet.

46. Salter, *Medieval Drama in Chester*, 65.

47. Craig, *Coventry Plays*, 99.

48. Young, op. cit., 14.

49. ibid., 15.

50. L. T. Smith, *York Plays*, xxxii.

51. Craig, *Coventry Plays*, 73, 99.

52. Kolve, *Corpus Christi*, 39.

53. ibid., 40. cf. Wickham, *Early English Stages* I, 314.

54. ibid., 45. cf. Wickham, *Shakespeare's Dramatic Heritage* (London 1969), 17.

55. See Martin Stevens' discussion of the elaboration of Latin plays, 'Illusion and Reality in the Medieval Drama', *College English* **32** (1971), 461–4.

56. Kolve, *Corpus Christi*, 48.

57. ibid., 51.

58. Wickham, *Early English Stages* I, 53–4.

59. For the most extensive discussion of the whole matter of the stations at York, including records not known to L. T. Smith, see Anna J. Mill, 'The Stations of the York Corpus Christi Play', *Yorkshire Archaeological Journal*, **37** (1951), 492–502 and app.

60. L. T. Smith, *York Plays*, xxxii.

61. Mill, op. cit., 493.

62. Anna Mill, in Appendix III of her article, presents schematically the stations listed in every known record, from which one can see which stations were always in use, and which varied. Appendix II, 520, shows amounts collected as rents for the stations from 1454–1569. This list 'shows clearly that the financial heyday of the York Corpus Christi plays was in the fifteenth century' (p. 498).

63. Alan Nelson, 'Principles of Processional Staging: York Cycle', *Modern Philology* **67** (1969–70), 303–20.

64. For an alternate view, see Alan Nelson, 'The Wakefield Corpus Christi Play', *RORD* **13–14** (1970–1), 221–33.

65. Craig, *ERD*, 205, gives the following account:

> An interesting circumstance appears in the records of 1426. William Melton, a Minorite Friar, tried to have the pageants postponed to the day after the Feast of Corpus Christi in order that the procession and the religious services of that day might have proper attention. He approved of the pageants but made a most reasonable appeal on the grounds of piety. He failed, however, for the plays continued to occupy Corpus Christi day, and the procession and the ceremonies were postponed until the day after.

Martin Stevens, who has examined the records, corroborates a verbal communication by Arthur Brown giving the correct version of what happened, adding that the reversal of the order used by Craig, with the plays being produced on the date of the feast, took place in the sixteenth century.

66. Smith, *York Plays*, xxxiv.

67. ibid., xxxvii.

68. It is perhaps worth remarking that the suggested sequence of events that I have just sketched out received some corroboration when first presented, see

RORD **12** (1969), 'Informal Minutes of Conference 53', 85–92. Martin Stevens reported then (91–2) that, while at work on an edition of the Towneley cycle, he had independently come to feel that Melton's visit in 1426 had crucial importance for the development of both cycles. He affirmed that after 1426 there were indeed two processions; the first was dramatic, and preceded Corpus Christi day, the second was religious, on the day itself. Once Professor Stevens had looked at the 1426 entry, he returned to Burton's *Ordo paginarum ludi Corporis Christi* printed on pp. xix–xxvii of Smith's edition of the plays. His conclusion was that the epitomes of the plays listed there are so completely out of consonance with the plays that survive that they must represent something else. Furthermore, Stevens reported that the second of Burton's lists, which Smith refers to, simply lists the names of the pageants, whereas the first represents an earlier stage of the York cycle. He had concluded from his study of Burton's lists that the first stage of the York cycle had been a series of *tableaux vivants* taken through the town, at least until 1425. Not all the plays Burton listed needed pageants; not all had speeches. Stevens suggested that some plays were put on in the afternoon during this period, after Mass had been celebrated.

69. See Anne C. Gay, 'The "Stage" and the Staging of the N-Town Plays', RORD **10** (1967), 135–40 for a discussion of this point; also Hosley, op. cit., 28–9 and n. 34. Hosley says, n. 34, that 'The term *station-to-station* production would be more 'medieval', since individual stops were sometimes called *stations*'. He himself prefers *stop-to-stop* as it seems to him to evoke the 'movement of a wagon' more effectively. Alan Nelson's term *True processional* he rejects, as do I, because of difficulties with the meaning of *True*. To the best of my knowledge Hosley was the first to propose the terms *station-to-station* and *stop-to-stop*.

70. Block, *Ludus Coventriae*, 39, s.d. l. 141. The Latin text reads: *Hic transit noe cum familia sua pro naui quo exeunte locum interludij sub intret statim lameth conductus ab adolescente et di* [*cit*].

71. For a full discussion of the significance of the episode, see Edmund Reiss, 'The story of Lamech and its place in medieval drama', *Journal of Medieval and Renaissance Studies* **2** (1972), 35–48.

72. The boy tells Lamech 'Vndyr yon grett busche mayster A Best do I se'. Block, *Ludus Coventriae*, 40, l. 166.

73. *Hic recedat lameth et statim intrat noe cum naui cantantes.* Ibid., 41, s.d. l. 197.

74. For the possible doctrinal reasons for including this episode, see the article by Reiss cited above, n. 69.

75. 'Staging the N-Town Cycle', *Theatre Notebook* **21** (1967), 122–38, 152–65.

76. Davis, *Non-Cycle Plays*, xxvii.

77. ibid., xxx–xxxi.

78. W. A. Mepham, 'The Chelmsford Plays of the Sixteenth Century', *The Essex Review* **56** (1947) 148–52, 171–8. I am indebted to Mrs A. Baugh, and to Professor John Murphy of the University of Colorado for bringing Mepham's work to my attention.

79. Dawson, *Plays and Players of Kent*, 202–11.

80. N. D. Shergold, *History of the Spanish Stage* (London 1967), 52–84.

81. ibid., 56.

82. ibid., 57–8.

Chapter 3. Dramatic possibilities

1. Hosley, 'Three Kinds of Outdoor Theatre', emphasizes the same quality in the pageant stage plays, 25–6.

2. *York Plays*, 112–17. Subsequent references are in the text. Orthography is normalized in the quotations.

3. *The Chester Plays* I, Ed. H. Deimling, EETS ES **62** (1892), 104–32. The running title given in the text is *The Nativity*, the actual title in the manuscript being *Pagina sexta de salutatione et nativitate Salvatoris Ihesu Christi*. Subsequent references here will be to *The Nativity*.

4. Salter, *Medieval Drama in Chester*, 45.

5. *The Digby Plays*, Ed. F. J. Furnivall, EETS ES **70** (1896), 127, l. 1923.

6. *Ludus Coventriae*, Ed. Block. Subsequent references are in the text.

7. The banns for this cycle, already referred to above, p. 16, do not list the plays covering the early events in the Passion sequence in the same order as these events are handled in the manuscript. The numbers in the margin of the manuscript containing these 'plays' do not appear at any clear breaks in the action, suggesting that the scribe was trying to square his text with the banns, but not doing so successfully. Dr Block in her edition entitles this body of material 'The Passion Play. I' (*Ludus Coventriae*, 225), which is an accurate and helpful title if readers are aware that it does not appear in the manuscript.

8. See Cameron and Kahrl, 'Staging the N-Town Cycle', 159–61. The following description differs in a few details from that proposed earlier, particularly in the elimination of the need for a Heaven scaffold.

9. For a thorough discussion of this miniature, including reproductions, see Southern, *Medieval Theatre in the Round*, 92–107.

10. Axton and Stevens, *French Plays*, 52 and 49 (diagram).

11. For the now classic discussion of the influence of medieval sermons on the cycle plays, see G. R. Owst, *Literature and Pulpit in Medieval England* (Cambridge 1933), 471–526.

12. Furnivall, *Digby Plays*, 81, l. 691.

13. A pair of doctors have been given speeches on the last leaf of the play. They add nothing to the action, and appear to be a later, inferior embellishment.

14. Smith, *York Plays*, 240–53.

15. M. James Young, 'The York Pageant Wagon', 14, noted these difficulties, but dismissed them by claiming that 'there are [no] more than three actors in addition to the disciples' performing in this play'. In fact, more are required at both locations (Gethsemane, and the palace of Caiphas).

Chapter 4. Character and verisimilitude

1. E. K. Chambers, discussing the effectiveness of the Wakefield Master, averred that 'There is no tenderness about him, and no impulse to devotion. He is a realist, even more than his contemporary of York [i.e., the so-called York "Realist"], a satirist with a hard outlook on a hard age' (*Eng. Lit. at the Close*, 37). Given Chambers' evident distaste for religious sentiment, this is commendation of a high order. For a study of the work of the York Realist, see J. W. Robinson, 'The Art of the York Realist', *Modern Philology* **60** (1963), 241–51.

2. For an excellent summary of the history of the term and its uses in European literature, see George J. Becker, *Documents of Modern Literary Realism* (Princeton 1963), introd. 3–38. Becker notes that 'the first use of the term "realism" in England occurred in a *Westminster Review* article on Balzac in 1853, although the phrase "realistic school" had been used but not defined in *Fraser's Magazine* two years earlier' (p. 7).

3. Professor Becker's definition of literary realism is as follows:

Realism denied that there was a reality of essences or forms which was not accessible to ordinary sense perception, insisting instead that reality be viewed as something immediately at hand, common to ordinary human experience, and open to observation. This attitude demanded that its readers and adherents abandon a host of preconceptions about human nature, about the purposes and mechanisms of the universe, and above all about the work of art. (p. 6)

4. For a discussion of the effect of Darwinism on the criticism of medieval drama, see O. B. Hardison, Jr, *Christian Rite and Christian Drama*, Essay I: 'Darwin, Mutations, and the Origin of Medieval Drama', 1–34.

5. *The Light of Common Day* (Bloomington, Ind., 1971), 18. It is quite possible that the survival of the Scottish common-sense school of philosophy in academic circles accounts for the general preference for realism to idealism in discussions of early drama. I am indebted to Professor Thomas Cooley of the Ohio State University for bringing Cady's work and Becker's anthology to my attention.

6. The approach to be followed in this chapter follows closely that proposed by Eleanor Prosser in *Drama and Religion in the English Mystery Plays* (Stanford, Calif., 1961). In her discussion of the problem of 'realism', Professor Prosser stated that 'The dramatic critic is not concerned with the realism of Cain's characterization as a Yorkshire farmer. His question relates to the character's function: Do the distinguishing traits that the playwright has given Cain make his murder of Abel and ensuing punishment dramatically probable?' (p. 60). Dramatic probability, however, as a critical tool itself assumes that the observable reality of common experience is still the primary criterion by which the play is to be judged. We will attempt to focus on the dramatic function of a character as well, but that function must relate to the larger meaning of the play, a meaning which in medieval drama asserts the validity of some transcendent truth. As it happens, in her insistence on the controlling influence of the doctrine of penance in the plays Professor Prosser is also concerned to assert a level of meaning beyond common experience.

7. Rossiter, *Early Times*, 50.

8. ibid., 69–70.

9. ibid., 72. An alternative use of the term 'realism' is provided by Martin Stevens in his important article 'Illusion and Reality in the Medieval Drama', *College English* 32 (1970–1), 448–64, esp. 460–3. Stevens rightly understands that the early drama is insisting on the absolute reality of the world of transcendence and eternity. This world he believes is made apprehensible by ritual, particularly the ritual of early liturgical drama. Later drama he would see as reproducing 'the theatrical illusion of reality' (p. 463). Misunderstanding of this development he traces to the naturalistic theatre of Ibsen, to which I have already had occasion to refer in our preliminary discussion of realism. The trouble with using the term

'realism' in the sense that Stevens is using it is that one ultimately has problems in differentiating between drama which asserts the existence of a transcendent reality, and drama which is concerned only to describe a mundane reality.

10. As we shall see, a translation of the original title as *The Purgation of Mary and Joseph* would have been a far more accurate title. For purposes of reference, Dr Block's title has been retained.

11. Rossiter, *Early Times*, 71.

12. See, for example, Kolve's rebuttal, *Corpus Christi*, 139.

13. The group of plays preceding *The Trial of Joseph and Mary*, plays eight to thirteen, are a self-contained unit, characterized by an extensive use of English stage directions calling for place-and-scaffold staging, and held together by a running commentary provided by the figure *Contemplacio*. In his opening speech, *Contemplacio* indicates that Mary's visit to Elizabeth will conclude the group of plays on the life of the Virgin; at the end of *The Visit to Elizabeth*, play thirteen, he states that that conclusion has been reached. Play fourteen, the *Trial*, contains Latin stage directions calling for a wagon stage, or at least a single scaffold.

14. In the *Protoevangelium*, Joseph and then Mary are sent away 'into the hill country' after taking the potion. In the *Pseudo-Matthew* they walk around the altar seven times. See M. R. James, *The Apocryphal New Testament* (London 1926), 44–5, 74.

15. See Morton W. Bloomfield, 'Beowulf, Byrhtnoth, and the Judgment of God: Trial by Combat in Anglo-Saxon England', *Speculum* 44 (1969), 545–59 for a general discussion of early ordeals, esp. 548–9. The ordeal of Joseph and Mary is of Bloomfield's type three, an ordeal to determine guilt or innocence, and is a *unilateral* ordeal, where one individual alone takes the test.

16. *Corpus Christi*, 8–32. Martin Stevens (op. cit., 450) shows that critical conceptions of what constitutes good drama have been heavily influenced by the conventions of the naturalistic theatre, itself a part of the Realistic movement, where 'The audience was asked to observe a recreation of life, seemingly unrehearsed, in a natural, photographically real setting. The best drama, under these circumstances, is that which asks its audience to forget the presence of the theatre altogether and to immerse itself totally in the illusion of reality created on stage'.

17. Bernard Spivack, *Shakespeare and the Allegory of Evil* (New York 1958), 180–1, underscores the conventional character of these two personifications of vice.

18. Edgar Hennecke, *New Testament Apocrypha*, Ed. Wilhelm Schneemelcher, Tr. R. McL. Wilson, vol. 1, 'Gospels and Related Writings' (Philadelphia 1963), 382.

19. This play embodies the doctrinal emphasis on repentance stressed by Professor Prosser in *Drama and Religion in the English Mystery Plays*, 19–42, though she does not use the play as an example.

20. A perception of this timeless appeal caused Gordon Honeycomb to include a modernized version of *The Trial of Joseph and Mary* in his adapted cycle *The Redemption* (London 1964).

21. *Mimesis*, Tr. Willard Trask (New York 1957), 138.

22. ibid., 138.

23. 'A real secularization does not take place until the frame is broken, until the secular action becomes independent; that is, when human actions outside of Christian world history, as determined by Fall, Passion, and Last Judgment, are

represented in a serious vein' (ibid., 140). Of this development we will have more to say in the concluding chapter.

24. As Frances A. Foster, the Editor for the *Northern Passion*, a major influence on the plays, has put it, 'the influence of early works like the *Cursor Mundi*, the *Northern Passion*, and the *Gospel of Nicodemus*, which can readily be traced on subsequent literature, does not imply actual transcription from a MS of the older poem on the part of the author, but rather a recollection of the older phrases as any one might employ in the case of works learned "by heart"'. *The Northern Passion*, EETS OS **147** (London 1916), introd., 101.

25. See A. C. Cawley, Ed., *The Wakefield Pageants in the Towneley Cycle* (Manchester 1958), xxi–xxv. References will be to this edition, and appear in the body of the text.

26. *A Pepysian Gospel Harmony*, Ed. Margery Coates, EETS OS **157** (London 1922). Gospel Harmonies date from as early as Tatian's *Diatessaron, c.* A.D. 160. They could be of two types, one arranging the text of the Gospels in four parallel columns, with the corresponding accounts contiguous, the other being a continuous narrative constructed out of the several accounts. The Pepysian Harmony is of the latter type. According to Dr Coates, the aim of its compiler, or compilers, was 'to present the life of Christ recorded in the four Gospels as an organic whole, set forth in the simplest language possible. Little therefore is omitted, little is added, and the deviations from the text of the original are mostly verbal and always in the direction of greater simplicity' (p. xlv).

27. There is no reference to the *Pepysian Harmony* either in Waldo F. McNeir's study of 'The Corpus Christi Plays as Dramatic Art', *Studies in Philology* **48** (1951), 601–28, or V. A. Kolve's chapter on 'The Passion and Resurrection in Play and Game', in *The Play Called Corpus Christi*, 175–205. Both, however, cite the *Northern Passion* as an important influence.

28. In this he is following John xviii, 13 (*Et adduxerunt eum ad Annam primum, erat enim socer Caiphae, qui erat pontifex anni illius*) and 24 (*Et misit eum Annas ligatum ad Caipham pontificem*).

29. See G. R. Owst, *Literature and Pulpit*, 510–11.

30. *Tunc expuerunt in faciem eius, & colaphis eum ceciderunt, alij autem palmas in faciem eius dederunt./Dicentes: Prophetiza nobis Christe, quis est qui te percussit?* (xxvi, 67–8). Latin quotations are from the Vulgate, English from the Rheims translation of 1582, or the Douai version of 1610, as being closer to the Vulgate than the King James version.

31. *Quia expedit, vnum hominem mori pro populo.*

32. *Sed nobis non licet interficere quemquam.*

33. See Kolve, *Corpus Christi*, 175–87, for an excellent discussion of the game aspects of the buffeting scene.

34. Annas in this scene reminds one strongly of the Turkish officer, played by Jose Ferrer, watching the beating of Lawrence in the film *Lawrence of Arabia*.

35. McNeir, 'Dramatic Art', 608. This generally fine sympathetic study is nevertheless marked by a preference for the more abstract devotional forms of early medieval art.

36. *Wakefield Pageants*, 122.

37. There are 398 lines in Smith's edition of the play, as opposed to 450 for the *Coliphizacio*.

38. See Robinson, 'York Realist', 245–6 for an alternative reading of this play.

39. ibid., 246–7.

40. *York Plays*, 255, l. 32. Subsequent references are within the text.

41. Let me add further that, having seen the play *The Dream of Pilate's Wife: Jesus before Pilate*, which Robinson praises ('York Realist', 246–7) as containing the most effective bedding-down scene, I must say that my own impression on each occasion was that there too the scene was characterized by extraneous irrelevant comedy which breaks the atmosphere of growing horror to no useful purpose, yet which could lead to Rossiter's theory of the Gothic double vision. It is not so much an example of double vision as an example of bad dramatic judgment on the part of the York Realist.

42. Thus Eleanor Prosser finds the N-Town version of the Crucifixion preferable to those of Towneley and York because it is shorter. For her, as for many others, 'the serious torture scenes seem to focus attention on the sensationalism of the acts of torture themselves, not on the suffering of the tortured' (*Drama and Religion*, 85). The question is not a matter of time, not whether the torturers go on too long. Even in the York *Crucifixion* there is very little waste dialogue in a play involving considerable complicated action.

43. English translation of *Literatur und darstellende Kunst im Mittelalter* (London 1970, hereafter cited as *Literature and Art*), 223–307.

44. *Literature and Art*, 246:

> The reason why attention was directed primarily to the Old Testament, and for the comparative neglect of the New, is to be found in Christ's own final teaching of the Apostles. Christ stated: '*all things must be fulfilled* which are written in the law of Moses, and in the prophets and in the psalms concerning me': [Luke xxiv, 44].... This was taken universally to be Christ's own *instruction* to study the Old Testament.

45. Here Pickering's discussion of Justus Lipsius' study *De Cruce*, 248–53, is particularly instructive as to the relation between 'History and Historia', i.e. what happened, and what tradition held as having taken place. For another study corroborating the essential role of tradition or 'auctoritee', in forming medieval attitudes toward the past, see also C. S. Lewis, *The Discarded Image* (Cambridge 1964).

46. 'It had the advantage of not inviting the objections of reverent craftsmen, whose ideas on what is mechanically feasible were always better respected than ignored' (*Literature and Art*, 240). For a full discussion of the differences between the two traditions of the Crucifixion, with quotations from two major sources the *Dialogue with the Holy Virgin* of Pseudo-Anselm for the Crucifixion *jacente cruce*, and the *Meditations* of Pseudo-Bonaventura for the Crucifixion *erecto cruce*, see pp. 237–45. Recognition of the existence of the two traditions, and of the use of only that involving the 'prostrate cross' in medieval English drama, has been common to such critics as Waldo McNeir and V. A. Kolve since it was pointed out by Beatrice Daw Brown in her edition of the *Southern Passion*, EETS OS 169 (London 1927), lxxiv–lxxxv.

47. *Foderunt manus meas & pedes meos: dinumerauerunt omnia ossa mea.* The Douai translation entitles this psalm 'Christ's Passion & effectes therof'. The gloss on the first words of the psalm reads as follows:

In respect of the end for which Christ suffered, this Psalme is intitled: for the morning enterprise: that is, for Christs glorious Resurrection, and other effectes of his Passion. Which holie Dauid by the spirite of prophecy so describeth here long before with diuers particular circumstances as the Euangelistes haue since historically recorded, that it may not vnfitly be called, *The Passion of Iesus Christ according to Dauid.*

The Second Tome of the Holie Bible, etc. (Lawrence Kellam, Douai 1610), 49.

48. *Exurge gloria mea, exurge psalterium & cithara: exurgam diluculo* (*Literature and Art,* 285–307). Whatever we may think of such 'Baroque imagery', Pickering undeniably establishes it as of great age, considerably antedating the cycle plays.

49. *York Plays,* 349, ll. 15–16. Subsequent references are in the body of the text.

50. One slight problem of interpretation arises due to the fact that the rubricator gives two successive speeches to the Second Soldier, where he should have only one. Smith's solution, to restore the succession of speakers one, two, three, four, is however surely not correct. It is at this point that the antiphonal quality of the speeches ends. I suggest as the correct ordering l. 100 assigned to the Fourth Soldier, ll. 102–4 to the Second, as written, and l. 105 to the First, as written. My interpretation of the action follows this ordering.

51. Rossiter, *Early Times,* 70.

52. McNeir 'Dramatic Art', 621, calls attention to the same context.

The apogee of medieval realism is reached in the Crucifixion, which represents the final and complete transformation of the universal symbolism of the liturgical office into the literal particulars of drama. In the later Middle Ages philosophical realism gave way to nominalism, the intellectual apprehension of the creed through scholasticism was replaced by an emotional and highly subjective *Weltanschauung* in the Dominican mystics, and the hieratic images of Romanesque art, monumental and aloof, receded before the ecstatic intimacy of late Gothic forms.

Chapter 5. Morality and farce

1. *Early English Stages* I, 262–73. A third group, the men's dramatic companies who produced the so-called 'mummers' plays', we must pass over for lack of space. For the most recent study of this topic, see Alan Brody, *The English Mummers and Their Plays* (Philadelphia 1969). Wickham's distinction between amateur and professional players provides a considerably more valuable approach to the nature of fifteenth-century dramatic activity than that followed by Muriel Bradbrook in the initial chapter of *The Rise of the Common Player* (London 1962), 1–38. Dr Bradbrook, whose gaze is fixed much more steadily on the late sixteenth century than on the fifteenth, stresses the multiplicity of dramatic activity in late medieval England to such an extent that confusion rather than enlightenment as to the origins of the professional companies results. The ensuing discussion follows closely Wickham's proposed reconstruction of the early development of professional acting companies in England.

2. Wickham, *Early English Stages* I, 267. David Bevington, *From Mankind to Marlowe* (Cambridge, Mass., 1962), 12, takes *histrio* as successor to *ministrallus* in the late fifteenth century.

3. *Plays and Players in Kent*, x–xi. See also E. K. Chambers, *MS* II, 232–3 for corroboration of this point. A contrasting point of view is expressed by Allardyce Nicoll in *Masks, Mimes and Miracles* (New York 1931), 150–1.

4. See, for example, Bevington, *Mankind to Marlowe*, 11–12; Bradbrook, *Common Player*, 22–4.

5. See Chambers, *MS* II, 262–3 for the text of this description.

6. Wickham, *Early English Stages* I, 264–9.

7. Chambers correctly saw that the term 'appears to be equally applicable to every kind of drama known to the Middle Ages' (*MS* II, 182). His own definition is as follows:

> I am inclined myself to think that the force of *inter* in the combination has been misunderstood, and that an *interludium* is not a *ludus* in the intervals of something else, but a *ludus* carried on between (*inter*) two or more performers; in fact, a *ludus* in dialogue. The term would then apply primarily to any kind of dramatic performance whatever. (II, 183)

Bevington, *Mankind to Marlowe*, follows Chambers in this definition. See also F. P. Wilson, *The English Drama 1485–1585*, Ed. G. K. Hunter (London 1969), 10–11.

8. Wickham, *Early English Stages* I, 266.

9. Chambers, *MS* II, 243.

10. Wickham, *Early English Stages* I, 267.

11. Unpublished accounts of the town of King's Lynn, Norfolk.

12. Unpublished accounts of King's Lynn. See also Chambers, *MS* II, 374.

13. Chambers, *MS* II, 256–7.

14. For a recent edition of the *Interludium de Clerico et Puellae*, see J. A. W. Bennett and G. V. Smithers, *Early Middle English Verse and Prose* (London 1966), 196–200; for *Dux Moraud*, see Davis, *Non-Cycle Plays and Fragments*, 106–13.

15. For a discussion of the amounts paid, see Dawson, *Plays and Players*, xviii; also my *Records of Plays and Players in Lincolnshire 1300–1585*, Malone Society Collections VIII (Oxford 1974), Introd..

16. The plays to be discussed are: *The Castle of Perseverance* (1400–25), *Mankind* (1465–70), *Everyman* (1495), and *Mundus et Infans* (1508).

17. See n. 7, above.

18. See G. R. Owst, *Literature and Pulpit*, 526–47.

19. W. R. Mackenzie, *The English Moralities from the Point of View of Allegory* (Boston, Mass., 1914), 9.

20. Mackenzie was not alone in emphasizing the presence of abstract characters as a distinguishing mark of these plays. Chambers, *MS* II, 153, remarked that 'The process of introducing abstractions into the miracle-plays themselves does not seem to have been carried very far. On the other hand, the moralities, if God and the Devil may be regarded as abstractions, admit of nothing else'.

21. Mackenzie, *The English Moralities*, 264.

22. For a discussion of the importance of costume in establishing character in these plays, see T. W. Craik, *The Tudor Interlude* (Leicester 1958), 49–92.

23. Robert A. Potter, 'The Form and Concept of the English Morality Play', (dissertation Claremont 1965), 190.

24. Chambers, *MS* II, 154.

25. The effect of this theory can be seen in Bernard Spivack's profuse references to the *Psychomachia* in his otherwise admirable study of *Shakespeare and the Allegory of Evil*.

26. Eccles, *Macro Plays*, 227, n. to l. 884.

27. This situation has been rectified by the excellent new anthology prepared by Edgar T. Schell and J. D. Shuchter, *English Morality Plays and Moral Interludes* (New York 1969). Citations will be to this version of the text as most easily available.

28. Compare Arnold Williams, *The Drama of Medieval England*, 155–7 and D. M. Bevington, *Mankind to Marlowe*, 15–18 for contrasting responses to the play. Professor Bevington's discussion is particularly important, as he takes *Mankind* to be representative of the form of early moral interludes. See also his discussion of *Mundus et Infans*, 116–24. I am throughout this discussion indebted to his thoughtful and perceptive analyses.

29. As Professor Bevington remarks, 'its simple design for two players, even if atypical, provides an admirably clear illustration of the principles to be pursued in later drama' (*Mankind to Marlowe*, 124). Bevington also notes (p. 117) that *Mundus et Infans* in its overall structure parallels the much longer *Castle of Perseverance*. Considering the excellent discussion of this structure by Richard Southern in *The Medieval Theatre in the Round*, it does not seem necessary here to discuss the structure of the *Castle* in detail.

30. See Chapter 2, n. 31, for discussion of this stage.

31. The Child subsequently underlines this concept by reminding the audience that 'when I was seven year of age/I was sent to the World to take wage' (ll. 115–16). The image is not that used at the play's opening, according instead with the figure of the Child as squire and then knight that is evolving through the course of the play, but the lack of personal responsibility for the initial fall is still central.

32. Note that the World does not leave the stage during this action, as Schell and Shuchter's stage directions imply.

33. Bevington, *Mankind to Marlowe*, 120.

34. cf. C. S. Lewis, *The Allegory of Love* (London 1936), 44–156.

35. For a discussion of the penitential tradition, see G. R. Owst, *Literature and Pulpit*, 526–36; Eleanor Prosser, *Drama and Religion*, 19–42: and, with particular reference to the Paternoster plays, Robert Potter, 'Form and Concept of the English Morality Play', 156–88. Potter's book is to be published by Routledge and Kegan Paul as *The English Morality Play*.

36. The debate of the Four Daughters of God in *The Castle of Perseverance* as to mankind's final resting place, which follows Mankind's death, is not a normal part of the interlude structure, and is not paralleled in other moral interludes. These normally end, at the latest, with the death of the central figure.

37. See Spivack, op. cit., *passim*, for a discussion of the Vice figure in the moral interludes.

38. ibid., 113–14.

39. Professor Spivack is particularly interested in demonstrating the pervasiveness of this characteristic in that it plays so important a part in Iago's character (ibid., 55–76).

40. *The Macro Plays*, Ed. M. Eccles, *Mankind*, 155, l. 29. Subsequent references are in the body of the text.

41. *Non-Cycle Plays and Fragments*, Ed. N. Davis, 73, l. 503.

Chapter 6. Of history and time

1. See Harold C. Gardiner, S.J., *Mysteries' End* (New Haven, Conn., 1946) for the fullest discussion of how the religious drama of the Middle Ages in England was systematically put down by Elizabeth's reforming bishops, largely to create a political settlement.

2. For these voyages and their impact on England, see Samuel Eliot Morison, *The European Discovery of America: The Northern Voyages* (New York 1971), 157–209 and 218–38. Morison quotes the passage from *The Interlude of the Four Elements*, 249–50, but believes it to be by an anonymous author.

3. For an account of this abortive voyage, see A. W. Reed, *Early Tudor Drama* (London 1926), 11.

4. Wilson, *The English Drama, 1485–1585*, 23.

5. ibid., p. 8.

6. See Stanley J. Kahrl, 'The Medieval Origins of the Sixteenth-Century English Jest-books', *Studies in the Renaissance* **13** (1966), 166–83.

7. The account of the structure, taken from Hall's *Chronicle*, is given in Reed, *Early Tudor Drama*, 19:

> 'there was builded a place like heaven, curiously painted with clouds, orbes, starres and hierarchies of angels. In the top of the pageant was a great type, and out of the type sodainly issued out of a cloud a fayre lady richely apparelled, and then all the minstrels which were in the pageant played and the angel sang, and sodainly again she was assumpted into the cloud, which was very curiously done, and aboute this pageant stode the apostles' whereof one said Latin verses' which Hall then gives.

8. ibid., 27.

9. O. B. Hardison, Jr, *Christian Rite and Christian Drama*, 290. The continued life of the cyclic view of history in Renaissance drama was originally proposed by E. Catherine Dunn as early as 1960 in her article 'The Medieval "Cycle" as History Play: an Approach to the Wakefield Plays', *Studies in the Renaissance* **7**, 76–89. Acceptance of her thesis has not, however, been rapid.

10. E. M. W. Tillyard, *Shakespeare's History Plays* (New York 1946), 92.

11. Irving Ribner, *The English History Play in the Age of Shakespeare* (London 1957), 28–9.

12. ibid., 30.

13. Lily B. Campbell, *Shakespeare's 'Histories': Mirrors of Elizabethan Policy* (San Marino, Calif., 1947).

14. For Ribner's rejection of the term 'chronicle play', see *English History Play*, 5–6.

15. Campbell, op. cit., 125.

16. See in this context Louis B. Wright's chapter on 'The Utility of History', in *Middle-class Culture in Elizabethan England* (repr. Ithaca, N.Y., 1958), 297–338.

17. Kolve, *Corpus Christi*, 48.

18. ibid., 58. The reference is to the *Middle English Sermons*, Ed. Woodburn O. Ross, EETS OS **209** (London 1940), 314.

19. Auerbach, *Scenes from the Drama of European Literature* (New York 1959), 29.

20. ibid., 53–4.

21. *Wakefield Pageants*, Ed. Cawley, 38, ll. 350–8.

22. ibid., 102–3.

23. Kolve, op. cit., 65–81, discusses a number of these interpretations.

24. ibid., 67.

25. *The Chester Plays*, pt. 1, Ed. Hermann Deimling, EETS ES **62** (London 1892), 83, ll. 465–76.

26. Ed. Noah Greenberg (New York 1959).

27. R. G. Collingwood, *The Idea of History* (London 1946), 49–50.

28. Dunn, 'The Medieval "Cycle" as History Play', 78–9.

29. St Augustine, *The City of God* XXII, 30, Tr. John Healey, Ed. R. V. G. Tasker (London 1945), ll. 407–8.

30. Kolve, *Corpus Christi*, 88–9.

31. For an excellent discussion of this play as an example of 'new and sophisticated techniques in the allegorizing of biblical narrative', see David Bevington, *Tudor Drama and Politics* (Cambridge, Mass., 1968), ch. 7 on 'The Royal Divorce and Suppression of the Monasteries', 86–95.

32. *John Bale's King Johan*, Ed. Barry B. Adams (San Marino, Calif., 1969) [I], 1107–19. Subsequent references are in the text.

33. See Bevington, *Tudor Drama and Politics*, 99, for further discussion of this point. Bevington defines the technique employed by Bale as 'historical analogy'.

34. Thora B. Blatt, *The Plays of John Bale* (Copenhagen 1968), 112. Barry B. Adams, in the introduction to the edition cited above, n. 32 (pp. 59–65), accepts Bale's historical conceptions as basically originating in the Apocalyptic thought patterns of 'sixteenth-century Protestant thinkers' (p. 59). This is too narrow a view.

35. E. K. Chambers, *MS* II, 222. Edward VI repealed the measure, but later lived to regret it.

36. Wilson, *The English Drama, 1485–1585*, 93–6.

37. Bevington, *Tudor Drama and Politics*, 112.

38. ibid., 109.

39. Chambers, *MS* II, 218–24.

40. Glynne Wickham, *Early English Stages 1300–1660* II, *1576–1660* pt 1 (London 1963), ch. 3, 54–97.

41. 'The Missing Parts of the Towneley Cycle', *Speculum* **45** (1970), 254–65.

42. Chambers, *The Elizabethan Stage* (London 1923), IV, 263.

43. Joel Hurstfield has indicated some of the limits to the control Elizabeth could impose on her people in *Liberty and Authority under Elizabeth I*, inaugural lecture (University College London, 12 May 1960), 9.

44. Gardiner, *Mysteries' End*, 70.

45. Campbell, 40–1.

46. Chambers, *MS* II, 361–2; 394; 379.

47. A. F. Leach, in *An English Miscellany* (London 1901), 227.

48. *The Dramatic Works of George Peele*, Ed. Charles T. Prouty; *David and Bethsabe*, Ed. Elmer Blistein (New Haven 1970), 175.

SELECTED BIBLIOGRAPHY

A. Bibliographies

Stratman, Carl. J., *Bibliography of Medieval Drama* (2nd ed., rev. and enlarged, 2 vols., New York 1972). The standard reference work. The new ed. focuses primarily on the needs of the student of medieval English drama though continental drama and Latin liturgical drama are also covered.

Zesmer, David M., *Guide to English Literature, From Beowulf through Chaucer and Medieval Drama*, (New York 1961). With extensive annotated bibliographies of the Old and Middle English periods by Stanley B. Greenfield. Excellent critical annotations included with selected bibliography.

B. Editions of individual works

Bale, John, *John Bale's King Johan*, Ed. Barry B. Adams (San Marino, Calif., 1969). For Bale's other works, see *The Writings of John Bale*, Ed. John S. Farmer (London, Early English Drama Society, 1907).

The Chester Plays, pt I, Ed. H. Deimling (EETS ES **62**, repr. London 1892); pt II, Ed. Matthews (EETS ES **115**, repr. London 1916).

The Chester Mystery Plays, Ed. Maurice Hussey (repr. London 1957). An adaptation of sixteen plays from the cycle.

The Cornish Ordinalia, Tr. Markham Harris (Washington 1969). The ed. and trans. by Edwin Norris (1859) is not generally available.

The Coventry Corpus Christi Plays: The Shearman and Taylors' Pageant and the Weavers' Pageant, Ed. Hardin Craig (EETS ES **87**, 2nd ed. London 1957). The 'true' Coventry plays.

The Digby Mysteries: The Killing of the Children, The Conversion of St Paul, Mary Magdalene, Christ's Burial and Resurrection, with an incomplete Morality of Wisdom, Who is Christ (Part of one of the *Macro Moralities*), Ed. F. J. Furnivall (New Shakespeare Society, London 1882, repr. Vaduz 1965). This ed. also reissued as *The Digby Plays* (EETS ES **70**, repr. London 1896).

Ludus Coventriae, or The Plaie called Corpus Christi, Ed. K. S. Block (EETS ES **120**, London 1922). The title of this play is a misnomer, and should be abandoned. Current practice favours 'The N-Town Cycle'.

The Macro Plays: The Castle of Perseverance, Wisdom, Mankind, Ed. Mark Eccles (EETS **262**, London 1969).

Non-Cycle Plays and Fragments, Ed. Norman Davis (EETS SS1, London 1970). Replaces ed. of same plays by O. Waterhouse (EETS ES **104**).

Skelton, John, *Magnyfycence*, Ed. Robert L. Ramsay (EETS ES **98**, repr. London 1908). The introduction contains a lengthy and important study of moral interludes.

The Towneley Plays, Ed. George England and A. W. Pollard (EETS ES **71**, repr. London 1897). Generally referred to now as the 'Wakefield Cycle'. The title 'Towneley' refers to the name of a former owner. This cycle contains the famous Second Shepherds' Play.

The Wakefield Pageants in the Towneley Cycle, Ed. A. C. Cawley (Manchester 1958). Contains six plays acknowledged to be written by the Wakefield Master.

The Wakefield Mystery Plays, Ed. Martial Rose (London 1961). A modernized version of the full cycle.

York Plays, Ed. Lucy Toulmin Smith (Oxford 1885; repr. New York 1963).

The York Cycle of Mystery Plays, Ed. J. S. Purvis (London 1957). A modernization of the original version. Different from the translation used as an acting version since 1951 at York.

For a full listing of the editions of moralities and interludes not covered in the texts listed above, see Bevington, David M., *From Mankind to Marlowe* (Cambridge, Mass., 1962), 274–8, and Craik, T. W. *The Tudor Interlude* (Leicester 1958), 142–149.

C. Anthologies

Adams, Joseph Q., *Chief Pre-Shakespearean Dramas* (Cambridge, Mass., 1924). Most inclusive, and thus most used. Badly needs revision, now being undertaken by David M. Bevington.

Armstrong, William A., *Elizabethan History Plays* (World's Classics **606**, London 1965). Includes Bale's *King John*.

Axton, Richard, and Stevens, John, Tr. *Medieval French Plays* (Oxford 1971). Includes *Le Jeu d'Adam* and *La Seinte Resureccion*.

Bennett, J. A. W., and Smithers, G. V., *Early Middle English Verse and Prose* (London 1966). Includes *Interludium de Clerico et Puella*.

Boas, F. S., *Five Pre-Shakespearean Comedies* (repr. World's Classics **418**, London 1934).

Browne, E. Martin, *Religious Drama 2. Mystery and Morality Plays* (New York 1958). Includes Browne's essay on 'Medieval Plays in Modern Production', together with a section on 'Scripts and Bibliography'.

Cawley, A. C., *Everyman and Medieval Miracle Plays* (New York 1959). A good classroom text where a composite cycle is desired.

Creeth, Edmund, *Tudor Plays* (New York 1966). A good selection of early sixteenth-century plays.

Davies, R. T., *The Corpus Christi Play of the English Middle Ages* (London 1972). Includes selections not often anthologized.

Gassner, John, *Medieval and Tudor Drama* (New York 1963). Texts heavily modernized, making anthology of questionable value.

Heilman, Robert B., *An Anthology of English Drama before Shakespeare* (New York 1952). Focuses more attention on Shakespeare's immediate predecessors than on early plays.

Hopper, Vincent F., and Lahey, Gerald B., *Medieval Mysteries, Moralities, and Interludes* (Woodbury, N. Y., 1962). Supplies 'the kind of eye-pleasing text and the kinds of reading and acting guides to which today's reader is accustomed. . . .'

Pollard, Alfred W., *English Miracle Plays, Moralities, and Interludes* (8th ed., rev., Oxford 1927). Longer plays heavily cut, introduction now much out-of-date. Of limited value.

Schell, Edgar T., and Shuchter, J. D., *English Morality Plays and Moral Interludes* (New York 1969). Best anthology of morality plays and interludes. Includes full text of *Castle of Perseverance*.

Thomas, R. G., *Ten Miracle Plays*. (York Medieval Texts, London 1966). An interesting selection from the cycles, intended as 'a useful primer for newcomers to the field'.

D. General Studies

Anderson, M. D., *Drama and Imagery in English Medieval Churches* (Cambridge 1963).

Bevington, David M., *From Mankind to Marlowe: Growth of Structure in the Popular Drama of Tudor England* (Cambridge, Mass., 1962).

—— *Tudor Drama and Politics: A Critical Approach to Topical Meaning* (Cambridge, Mass., 1968).

Boas, Frederick S., *University Drama in the Tudor Age* (1914; repr. New York 1966).

Brody, Alan, *The English Mummers and their Plays: Traces of Ancient Mystery* (Philadelphia 1969).

Chambers, E. K., *The Mediaeval Stage* (2 vols, London 1903).

—— *English Literature at the Close of the Middle Ages* (corr. repr., Oxford 1947).

Craig, Hardin, *English Religious Drama of the Middle Ages* (London 1955).

Craik, T. W., *The Tudor Interlude: Stage, Costume, and Acting* (Leicester 1958).

Farnham, Willard, *The Medieval Heritage of Elizabethan Tragedy* (1936; corr. repr. Oxford 1956).

Gardiner, H. C., S. J., *Mysteries' End: An Investigation of the Last Days of the Medieval Religious Stage* (Yale Studies in English **103**, 1946; repr. Hamden, Conn., 1967).

Harbage, Alfred, *Annals of English Drama, 975–1700: An Analytical Record of All Plays, Extant or Lost, Chronologically Arranged and Indexed by Authors, Titles, Dramatic Companies*, etc. (rev. ed. by S. Schoenbaum, London 1964). Subscribers are mailed free supplements with the compliments of Professor Schoenbaum.

Hardison, O. B., Jr, *Christian Rite and Christian Drama in the Middle Ages: Essays in the Origin and Early History of Modern Drama* (Baltimore 1965).

Hunniningher, Benjamin, *The Origin of the Theatre* (Amsterdam 1955).

Kinghorn, A. M., *Medieval Drama* (London 1968).

Kolve, V. A., *The Play Called Corpus Christi* (Stanford 1966).

Owst, G. R., *Literature and Pulpit in Medieval England: A Neglected Chapter in the History of English Letters & of the English People* (2nd ed., rev., Oxford 1961).

Prosser, Eleanor, *Drama and Religion in the English Mystery Plays: A reevaluation* (Stanford 1961).

Righter, Anne, *Shakespeare and the Idea of the Play* (London 1962, Penguin ed. 1967).

Rossiter, A. P., *English Drama from Early Times to the Elizabethans: Its Background, Origins, and Developments* (London 1950).

Roston, Murray, *Biblical Drama in England from the Middle Ages to the Present Day* (London 1968).

Salter, F. M., *Mediaeval Drama in Chester* (Toronto 1955, repr. New York 1968).

Southern, Richard, *The Medieval Theatre in the Round: A Study of the Staging of the Castle of Perseverance and Related Matters* (London 1957).

Spivack, Bernard, *Shakespeare and the Allegory of Evil: The History of a Metaphor in Relation to His Major Villains* (New York 1958).

Taylor, Jerome, and Nelson, Alan, *Medieval English Drama: Essays Critical and Contextual* (Chicago and London 1972).

Wickham, Glynne, *Early English Stages, 1300 to 1660*: vol. I, *1300–1576*; vol. II, pt 1, *1576–1600*; vol. II, pt 2, *1576–1600* (London 1959–72).

Williams, Arnold, *The Drama of Medieval England* (East Lansing, Mich., 1961).

Wilson, F. P., *The English Drama, 1485–1585*, Ed. G. K. Hunter (London 1969).

Woolf, Rosemary, *The English Mystery Plays* (Berkeley and Los Angeles 1972).

Young, Karl, *The Drama of the Medieval Church* (2 vols, Oxford 1933).

INDEX